THE Crafted garden

THE
Crafted
garden

Stylish projects inspired by nature

Louise Curley
photography by
Jason Ingram

F

FRANCES LINCOLN LIMITED
PUBLISHERS

Frances Lincoln Ltd
74–77 White Lion Street
London N1 9PF
www.franceslincoln.com

The Crafted Garden
Copyright © Frances Lincoln
   Limited 2015
Text copyright © Louise
   Curley 2015
Photographs copyright ©
   Jason Ingram 2015, except
   those listed on page 176

First Frances Lincoln edition
   2015
Designed by Becky Clarke

A catalogue record for this
book is available from the
British Library

ISBN 978-0-7112-3629-5

Printed in China

9 8 7 6 5 4 3 2 1

Contents

Introduction

The Crafted Garden is a collection of craft projects and techniques inspired by my garden, plants and the great outdoors. Following the seasons it includes some of my favourite ways to celebrate nature. By combining fresh ideas with time-honoured techniques, I will show you how to ditch mass-produced decorations and gifts and find ideas in the natural and handmade.

Nature tables at school were my first introduction to the diversity, detail and incredible beauty of the natural world. While my teachers seemed to have a preference for a motley collection of taxidermy animals and birds, it was the shells and leaves, unusual seed heads and feathers that captured my imagination. I would spend hours poring over the *Brambly Hedge* books so beautifully and intricately illustrated by Jill Barklem, which were inspired by the ancient woodland of Epping Forest in Essex, UK. In them were the stories of mice with names such as Poppy and Teasel, who lived in the trees and hedgerows. Jill would gather plant material and fill her studio to inspire her drawings. I was, and still am, mesmerized by the detail of her illustrations of houses built into trees with kitchens laden with crab apples, mice squirrelling away nuts and berries, and rooms decorated for winter using holly and mistletoe. Now I have my own nature table on the desk where I write. There are shells from holidays in Cornwall and Scotland, fossils, prettily striped pebbles and a vase of sparkling honesty (*Lunaria*) seed pods. All are reminders of time spent in some of my favourite places. I have always loved making things too. As a child, if given some glue, a cardboard box and some pretty paper and

Gather together seed heads from the garden and display beside finds from country walks and the seaside for your own nature table.

The intricate beauty of opium-poppy seed heads makes them stunning crafting material.

I would be happy for hours. Now, whenever I get stuck for creativity, I try to channel the thoughts and freedom of the seven-year-old me who created a collage of a fish from lentils, sweet wrappers and a verruca plaster! Today, it is my garden and the countryside that provide the inspiration and source material for my craft projects.

Several years ago I became aware of the environmental cost of imported cut flowers. It spurred me on to grow my own cut flowers and write my first book – *The Cut Flower Patch* – about celebrating seasonality through home-grown flowers. While writing that book I discovered so many ways in which I could use nature to make my home look beautiful that ideas for *The Crafted Garden* started to form.

I wanted to be able to combine my love of nature and crafting to decorate my home in a sustainable, unique way, which captured the seasons. I have always decorated my home at Christmas with natural materials – there have been sprigs of holly (*Ilex*) and garlands of ivy (*Hedera*) and recently I have developed a bit of an obsession with pine (*Pinus*) cones. But then I came across other plants that I could be growing in my garden or be picking from the hedgerows, and I found there was something really rewarding about using nature to enhance my home.

Sometimes my decorations can be as simple as bringing newly bought plants indoors for a while and displaying them in an attractive way while they are at their peak, to appreciate them up close. This works particularly well with spring-flowering plants with their exquisitely small blooms, which deserve closer inspection. Often, when new plants are bought, they can languish in their pots for weeks before they are planted up. It struck me as a pity that I did not get to appreciate them more, so I started to bring them indoors for a week or so, which was a much better introduction to them than abandoning them in my greenhouse. And, as my interest in crafting with natural material has grown, I have devised ways in which to use flowers and seed heads from my cut flower patch or from foraged finds from the countryside. This can mean drying flowers in order to create a midsummer wreath, using bark or stems to make pretty vases or creating a garland from autumn leaves.

You might want to conjure up the feeling of a rural idyll, but you do not need to live in one – parks and hedgerows can be great sources of natural crafting material, particularly in autumn and winter. And if you are lucky enough to have a garden or allotment there are so many plants that can be grown easily, which will provide you with a ready source of natural crafting material. First and foremost the plants should look good in your garden, but if they can also be dried, are wonderfully fragrant, have pretty flowers which can be preserved, form stunning seed heads or have fabulous autumn leaves then so much the better. By combining these gems with bits and pieces collected from woodland walks or beachcombing trips, you can make decorations that can be both beautiful and kind to the planet.

ENDLESS POSSIBILITIES

The Crafted Garden is a collection of some favourite techniques and projects that I have discovered and used, and they combine my love of nature and crafting. I am not a florist and I do not have the nimblest of fingers, but I will show you that it is possible, with a little imagination, to make simple, quirky and individual projects using nature as your inspiration. Instead of filling a vase with imported flowers for a dinner party, why not decorate the table with beautiful, edible plants? If you are struggling to think of a house-warming gift or birthday present for a friend, you could propagate some of your own plants and give them in pretty hessian

pouches (see page 90). We all tend to spend too much time in front of computer screens so the projects that require a spot of foraging are the perfect excuse to get outdoors. What could be better in autumn and winter than a walk in the woods collecting pretty lichen twigs and pine cones followed by an afternoon spent making decorations for Christmas? And many of the ideas are perfect for getting children hooked on plants.

So next time you are out walking in the countryside or pottering around your garden, take inspiration from what you see and try a spot of crafting with nature.

Use nature to decorate your home, to make gifts for gardening friends and to celebrate the changing seasons.

A few simple bits are all you need for your crafting toolbox. Keep a lookout for pretty threads and twines, and store them in an old shoebox.

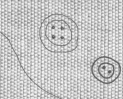

Crafting tips and kit

I have tried to keep the tools needed to a minimum. I love creating projects that can be replanted or that can be put straight on to the compost heap when they are no longer needed. As a result I like to use natural twines and cords such as hemp, jute or flax. An assortment of wire and a glue gun are essential parts of my crafting tool kit too. Both help to make more robust creations, which can be stored and reused in following years. Projects such as the seasonal wreaths can be easily dismantled and composted once you have finished with them, and any wire can be reused. Have a look at the resources section for a list of suppliers (see page 168).

FLORISTS' WIRE

You may come across the letters 'SWG' when looking for florists' wire. This means Standard Wire Gauge and refers to the imperial numbering which grades the thickness of wire. It can be quite easy to be bamboozled by the variety and sizes of wire available. The important thing to remember is that the higher the gauge the thinner the wire. Thinner wire is more malleable and less obtrusive, but is not substantial enough for projects that require more strength. For basic projects a thin-gauge wire (26–28SWG; 0.46–0.38mm) and a medium-gauge wire (20–24SWG; 0.91–0.56mm) should be sufficient.

The other choice is stub or reel wire. Stub wire comes in pre-cut lengths, while reel wire is one long length wrapped around a reel. I use both. A medium-gauge reel wire is particularly useful for wrapping the bases of wreaths, which need some support and strength. You can also cut it into sections to create your own stub wire. Stub wire, which is convenient for wiring posies, tends to come in a greater selection of sizes. Florists' wire is available in green, black and brown, and the very finest wire in silver, which is particularly useful for wiring posies together.

FLORAL TAPE

You will find floral tape useful if you want to disguise stems wrapped with wire, and it will give your projects a more professional finish. It takes a bit of practice to master floral tape, but it is well worth it. Floral tape is available in brown and shades of green. I prefer the brown tape as it blends in with most natural material. It is best to break off sections of tape about 15cm/6in long – if any longer or left on the roll, it will be cumbersome to work with. The tape is strangely not sticky when you first come to use it – the warmth of your fingers will activate the glue. It is also a good idea to stretch the tape gently, holding both ends and carefully pulling, because this makes it more pliable and so easier to cover the wire. There are more tips on how to use floral tape in the headdress project on page 76.

GLUE GUNS

I prefer to create projects that are as natural as possible, but a hot-glue gun does open up the crafting possibilities. You do not need to spend a lot of money on one (see Favoured resources, page 168), and it is easy to use. The key with hot-glue guns is to remember that the bonding between two surfaces occurs when the glue cools, so you need to work quickly once the glue has been applied to attach items to where you want them to stick. Press and hold in place for about 30 seconds. I have found the glue to be quite forgiving so if you make a mistake peel off the glue before it has fully set and start again. The glue will continue to set, so when it is completed put your project to one side for a day or so to allow it to harden.

Take care not to burn yourself with hot glue, and supervise any children using glue guns.

CONTAINERS

Most of the containers I use in this book are meant only as temporary homes for the plants while you display them indoors. In the long term most plants prefer to stretch out their roots into a bigger space, either into the soil or a larger container outdoors. Despite this, it is still worth bearing a few things in mind when choosing a temporary container.

It is important to consider the size of your plant's root ball and whether it will fit into your chosen container, as it is not really feasible to reduce the size of the root ball without potentially damaging your plant.

Plants will be happy in a container with no drainage holes for only a very short period of time before their roots are starved of air, and water that is not able to drain away over a prolonged time will cause roots to rot. There are a few exceptions (see Terrariums, page 28; see also HOW TO: Force bulbs, page 162). If you want to display your plants for only a day or so, perhaps for a party, then that is fine, but

for any longer period you would need to add some drainage holes. Alternatively plant into a 'sleeve', which could be a simple plastic or terracotta pot that has drainage holes and then slip this inside the more attractive pot you want to use for display. The Victorians called these cache pots.

Think about where you will be placing the container and whether the surface may be scratched or damaged by water or compost from the base of your container. The 'sleeve' solution mentioned above is ideal if this is an issue, or you could protect your furniture and catch any spills by using a pretty tray, plate or piece of stone that complements your display.

There is a wealth of choice when it comes to material, colour and style of container. Metal containers work well with a whole range of plants. Reclamation yards, flea markets and charity shops are treasure troves for old tins, zinc baths and kitchen pots, which can make quirky homes for your plants. Wood is a great choice as it creates a good root environment for the plants to grow in, and if you are feeling crafty it is easy to make a simple container from old pallets. Dainty teacups make for sweet but very temporary displays, because they lack drainage holes. Scouring flea markets and vintage shops is a fun way to while away an afternoon, while reusing old finds adds a quirky, individual touch to your natural crafting and is generally much better for the environment.

PLANTING TIPS

Even if your project is providing only a temporary home for plants it is still important to give them the best growing conditions. By following the tips below you will keep your plants happy and healthy for the purposes of your project, and if you plan for them to have a life afterwards it will keep them in the best condition for planting out into your garden.

- It has always been horticultural practice to fill the bottom of pots with a few crocks – broken bits of terracotta pot – to aid drainage. In recent years however trials have disputed whether this actually has any effect and even has suggested that it might be detrimental to the plant. I tend not to bother but, if you want to put something at the bottom of a small pot to prevent the compost from falling through the drainage holes, use newspaper or kitchen paper.
- For short stays in containers, multipurpose compost is fine. When you come to plant outdoors into the garden, enrich the planting hole with some home-made garden compost or leafmould, depending on the specific requirements of the individual plant. If you are planting into a container for a more permanent home, then use a soil-based, peat-free John Innes No. 3 compost, which will provide more stability, will not dry out as quickly as a multipurpose compost and will release nutrients slowly over a longer period of time. Some plants such as alpines or succulents require very good drainage so mixing the compost with horticultural grit will help with this (see Potting mix for alpines, page 36).
- If you are using a planting sleeve (see Containers, page 12), remove it from the outer container, water your plants thoroughly and then allow the pot to drain for ten minutes or so before placing it back within the decorative container.
- For containers without any drainage holes, add a layer of small pebbles about 2.5cm/1in deep, to the base. This will provide somewhere for water to drain into and mean the plant roots are not sitting in water. And, if you are using a container with no drainage holes for more than a few days, say for planting bulbs for forcing or using a terrarium, add some horticultural charcoal (otherwise known as biochar) to the mix. Stagnant compost does have a tendency to smell a little unpleasant, and the addition of charcoal will keep it fresh.
- To finish off your projects cover any exposed compost with a layer of fine grit, small pebbles or moss (harvested from your garden). Not only will this look much more attractive than bare compost but it will also help to retain moisture around the plant.

Your choice of container is key in creating an attractive display. Think about materials, colours and textures, and plants to go in it.

Foraging and aftercare

Protecting and conserving our native flora are crucial if future generations are to have the opportunity to appreciate our natural environment too. In the past the foraging of certain plants has impacted greatly on their populations, so much so that plants such as the primrose (*Primula vulgaris*), a popular flower to pick and sell in the late nineteenth and early twentieth centuries, was threatened in the wild.

For me a spot of foraging, when I pick the occasional flower or tree branch, scour the woodland floor for fascinating pine cones or comb a beach for pretty shells, is all part of learning to appreciate and respect nature. I am a great believer that if we immerse ourselves in the natural world we are much more likely to care for and want to protect it. A 'do not touch' approach, particularly where children are concerned, can make us feel alienated from a world from which we are increasingly losing contact. However, while some plants grow in abundance and quickly, others, particularly wild flowers, are on the decline and plants such as mosses and lichens can take years to grow. So foraging is all about common sense really, and knowing a few rules means it can be enjoyed safely without damaging the environment.

For more information consult the Botanical Society of the British Isles' Code of Conduct (www.bsbi.org.uk/Code_of_Conduct.pdf). The charity Plantlife (http://plantlife.org.uk) is a fantastic source of information, as is your local Wildlife Trust (www.wildlifetrusts.org).

Guidelines for foragers

- Never uproot plants from the wild.
- Pick only plants you recognize and that are numerous, and take only small amounts for personal use.
- Do not pick from Sites of Special Scientific Interest (SSSIs) and nature reserves.
- Ask the landowner's permission.
- Be careful not to damage surrounding plants while foraging.
- Windfalls such as weeping birch and lichen-covered stems are perfect.
- Never remove lichen or moss from where it is growing.
- Take inspiration from nature. Many of our native wild plants can be grown easily in our gardens. Buy plants and seeds from specialist growers. Picking from your garden is always preferable to gathering from the wild.
- Some plants are protected and it is illegal to harvest them. Check these before you plan your foraging trips. If in doubt, do not pick.
- Some plants are poisonous. Take a good field guide with you. It is very easy to mistake certain plants.
- Wear gloves to protect against prickles, thorns and irritant saps.

OPPOSITE Forage for plants that grow in abundance, thereby leaving plenty for wildlife.

BRINGING PLANT MATERIAL INDOORS

Flowers and foliage are fabulous ways of creating a beautiful home, but it is important to consider the other members of your household when selecting the plant material you bring indoors. If you have small children or pets it is worth remembering that quite a lot of plants are poisonous. Perhaps because we see them every day we forget about their toxic properties or maybe we never realized their potency in the first place. The list of plants that could cause harm is too long to include here, but the following websites have all the information you should need: www.rhs.org.uk/advice/Profile?pid=524; and www.dogstrust.org.uk/help-advice/factsheets-downloads/factsheetpoisonoussubstances09.pdf.

Poisoning is rare but here are a few tips to protect your family and pets:

- Store bulbs and seeds away from children and pets.
- Tidy up as your plants fade, so berries, pollen and seeds are not lying around where they could be eaten.
- Display plant material that may be a problem out of reach of young children and pets.
- Teach children of the dangers, and train pets not to eat plants.

Allergies too can pose a problem. Grass and tree pollen are the most likely sources of irritation. I suffer from hay fever, and growing and arranging ornamental grasses does make my symptoms worse. I am happy to make that choice but I would not want to inflict it on others, so bear it in mind if you want to use this sort of material.

OPPOSITE When you grow your own flowers you can cut fresh blooms all summer long.

LOOKING AFTER CUT FLOWERS

Whether you devote a few beds especially to growing cut flowers or you simply pick a few blooms from the plants growing in your garden, it is worth giving the cut flowers some special care once picked, to get the most from them.

Guidelines for cutting

- If you can, harvest cut flowers in the early morning or evening. This is when plants are most full of water, with strong, upright stems, and are least likely to wilt.
- Use clean, sharp secateurs to cut the stems and make a diagonal cut to expose more of each stem.
- Put the stems into a bucket of cool water immediately.
- Ideally place your flower bucket somewhere cool and shady for at least a few hours or overnight.
- Recut stems to fit your vase and arrangement.
- Plant food is unnecessary.
- Change the water in your vase every few days.
- Some flowers, such as poppies (*Papaver*) and roses, benefit from having the ends of their stems seared in boiling water for 20–30 seconds to stop them shedding petals or wilting.
- When trimming woody stems, make a vertical cut of about 2.5cm/1in from the base up the centre of each stem, to expose more stem to the water.
- Flowers will last longest if kept somewhere cool. A baking hot windowsill will see them fade much more quickly.

Spring crafts

Introduction

The first glimmers of spring are hugely welcome after the grey and brown palette of winter. Emerging spring flowers with their freshness and vibrancy of new life contrast so starkly with the past months. The pace of change in the garden and the countryside is palpable as buds break, shoots appear and flowers burst open. You can feel and smell the energy of the sun when you walk through a woodland on those first warm days of spring as the sap starts to rise.

Deciduous woodlands and hedgerows come into their own at this time of year and provide inspiration for both the garden and home. The zingy green of the trees and hedges bursting into life and a pretty sprinkling of colourful flowers fill the heart with joy. Many of these wild flowers look perfect when planted in the garden along with their cultivated cousins. They do not have to be just planted outdoors; many make great cut flowers and others can be appreciated indoors for a few weeks in pretty containers while they are in their prime. The great advantage in bringing these early flowering plants into your home is that they give you the opportunity to appreciate them up close.

Bluebells (top left) and tulips (above) are some of the first colourful blooms of spring.

Eggshell vases
with a birch nest and spring flowers

Eggs are a symbol of birth and have become inextricably linked with Easter. I remember making all sorts of crafty projects using eggs when I was a child, so I was inspired to create something a little more grown-up and combine it with my love of cut flowers. This little decoration would make a perfect centrepiece for an Easter family feast, but it would work equally as well when displayed on a side table or windowsill. It is very easy to create and, when you are finished with it, it can go on the compost heap.

Making the nest

Take strips of bendy birch twigs and weave together to create a circle. It should be possible to wend in the ends to secure the nest shape, but, if you need to, use a little piece of florists' wire or hemp cord. Add further strips, weaving them in to fill out the nest.

Preparing the eggshell vases

Puncture the pointy end of each duck or hen egg, using a needle. Then carefully remove small pieces of the eggshell, to open it up. Empty the contents of each egg into a bowl and use these later, for an omelette or some baking. Rinse each eggshell with a little soapy water.

Forming the egg stands

Cut down sections of an egg box as supports for each egg when placed inside the nest. They should be small enough not to be seen once inside the nest.

Assembling the display

Fill your eggshells with water and place in position on their egg-box stands. Then set the birch nest over the top and add your flowers to each shell.

TOP TIP

These eggshell vases are only small and do not hold much water so top them up every day.

Grape hyacinths

WHY? These small bulbs bear flower heads that really do look like a bunch of grapes. The classic colour of grape hyacinths (*Muscari*) is blue, but look out for white varieties and the unusual yellow/brown *M. macrocarpum* 'Golden Fragrance'. They work well edging paths, in pots and as cut flowers for small vases.

HOW? Plant the bulbs from early to mid-autumn, to three times their depth. Once established, they will send up a clump of grass-like leaves in autumn, followed by flowers in mid-spring.

Forget-me-nots

WHY? The perfect accompaniment to spring bulbs are the tiny flowers of forget-me-nots (*Myosotis*), which create a hazy effect around the base of daffodils and tulips. They add a naturalistic feel to a garden and are very easy to grow. They will last up to a week in a vase. Forget-me-nots also look perfect when preserved in a home-made flower press.

HOW? Their ideal growing conditions are dappled shade and moist soil rich in leafmould. However they are quite tolerant plants and will do remarkably well in drier, sunnier spots.

Primroses

WHY? For me these are the quintessential spring flower. Typically, primroses (*Primula vulgaris*) bloom from early to mid-spring but in a mild winter you may have them flowering at Christmas. They make one of the best spring cut flowers, as they last up to a week. The flowers are edible too.

HOW? Primroses like a sunny spot but prefer shade from summer sunshine so their perfect planting site is under deciduous trees and shrubs and in semi-shady borders. Mature plants can be found at specialist wildflower nurseries or at garden centres with a native plants section. Once established, they are easy to increase by division or fresh seeds (see page 26).

Celebrate the end of winter by bringing spring flowers indoors to decorate your home.

Growing primroses

Primroses are a must for any celebration of spring. You are unlikely to have much success with shop-bought seeds as primrose seed germinates best when sown fresh and straight from the plant. Do not let this put you off growing them though. Buy in a few plants from a nursery with a wild plant section or from a specialist wildflower grower, and nature will do the hard work for you. It will not be long before you spot young primrose seedlings sprouting in cracks in your garden path or in the soil around your established plants. Gently lift these youngsters, being careful not to damage their roots, and put into small pots filled with compost. Grow on somewhere shady until they are more substantial plants before planting in their new home.

You can also increase your primrose stock by division. This entails splitting a plant into smaller sections and replanting them. Dividing a plant can seem a bit brutal, but it is actually good for it and should be done anyway every few years to invigorate it. When your primroses have finished flowering in mid- or late spring, dig up a clump and gently prise it apart, into smaller pieces. Make sure each new section has a good amount of roots attached to it. Replant elsewhere, having enriched each planting hole with a little compost, either home-made or multipurpose; then water in.

Primroses are a must-have plant for even the smallest of gardens. They flower from late winter right through to late spring and make long-lasting cut flowers.

Sowing forget-me-nots

Their name is rather apt as I often do forget to sow them. They are biennials so should be started off from late spring through to midsummer. Scatter them into a seed tray filled with multipurpose compost. Cover the seeds with a thin layer of compost. Water gently with a small watering can or one with a rose on the end of the spout, so as not to disturb the seeds. Label with the name and sowing date and place somewhere warm and sunny – a greenhouse, cold frame or windowsill is perfect. Forget-me-nots should germinate in 7–10 days.

Check the seedlings regularly, and water if the compost is drying out; also look out for slugs. When the seedlings have two sets of leaves – the seed leaves and the first set of real or true leaves – carefully prick them out and pot on into smaller pots filled with multipurpose compost. While holding each seedling by a seed leaf, lever out the seedlings from the tray, using a plant label. If a seed leaf gets damaged it is not a problem; it is important however not to injure the stem and the true leaves. Water the transplants, and put their pots somewhere sunny but sheltered from the midday sun.

By early autumn they will have formed good-sized plants, which can be planted out into the garden or a dedicated cut flower patch, ready for spring flowering.

The great thing about forget-me-nots is that they will self-sow once they are established, so even if you do forget to sow some you will find clumps popping up here and there.

Other biennials that can be grown from seed to provide you with spring blooms include honesty, sweet rocket and wallflowers.

Sprinkle the seeds over the surface and then cover with a thin layer of compost.

Terrariums

If you are short on time and space, your houseplants tend to die through neglect or you are looking for a way to inspire children to appreciate plants, a terrarium could be the answer. Creating a mini garden encased in glass first became popular in Victorian Britain thanks to Nathaniel Ward and his mini greenhouse – the Wardian case. This essential piece of equipment for plant hunters of the day allowed them successfully to bring plants home from across the globe. Soon, Wardian cases became popular with plant-mad people in the nineteenth century, but they fell out of favour in the twentieth century until a resurgence in interest in the 1970s and 1980s in the form of bottle gardens. I was fascinated by these tiny worlds as a child; there was something quite intriguing about creating a specimen of the plants and highlighting their beauty behind glass.

RECYCLE AND REPURPOSE

I think it is perhaps time for a bit of a revival of the terrarium. They fit perfectly with the ideas of recycling and repurposing. Have a rummage through your kitchen cupboards or take a trip to a flea market or vintage shop in search of the perfect container. Plain glass is what you are looking for in a container that will be large enough to take your plant/s and the growing mix of compost, biochar (see box, opposite) and pebbles. Large pickling jars, old-fashioned sweet jars and preserving jars are all excellent. You can even try a glass cloche standing on a pretty base such as a cake stand or tray.

SUITABLE PLANTS

A true terrarium is sealed with a lid, and the moist, humid environment created inside is perfect for mosses, tiny hostas, lichens and ferns. Once planted, watered and sealed, your terrarium will need little attention. The moisture inside will be sufficient to keep the plants watered, and all you need to do is to remove the lid every week or so for a few hours to provide a little ventilation. After six months, or perhaps a year, you may need to remove your plants and divide them if your terrarium is looking a little crowded. Take this opportunity to refresh the compost and biochar.

Other looser interpretations of terrariums are based on open glass containers. These work perfectly for succulents, which need dry conditions to replicate their natural environment. Or why not try the exotic and fascinating carnivorous plants? These need to be grown in an unsealed environment so they can feed on any passing flies. You can even use a glass jar for a temporary display, perhaps for a dinner party.

Victorian engraving of a Wardian case

Fritillaria

WHY? Snake's head fritillary (*Fritillaria meleagris*) must be one of the most striking and unusual of all spring flowers. With its multitude of common names including leper lily, frawcup and minety bell, this is a plant that has found a way into our hearts. And it is no real surprise. Snake's head fritillary has a delicate beauty and elegance, with its thin stems and nodding, lantern-like flowers. Their chequerboard pattern is distinctive, and while the petals – the hue of the darkest red wine – can appear a tad dull, they look like a well-lit stained-glass window when the sunlight catches them.

HOW? Snake's head fritillary prefers soils that flood in winter, and colonies of them can often be seen in meadows near rivers. They can be grown quite happily in a garden, though, as long as the soil does not dry out. Growing them from bulbs can be a bit hit and miss, but you can find flowering plants easily enough at garden centres and plant fairs in spring. Enjoy them for a few days indoors – perhaps in an open terrarium – before planting them into the ground.

Lily-of-the-valley

WHY? There is a pure beauty to the tiny, fragrant, bell-shaped flowers of this woodland plant – a traditional flower of May Day celebrations. Lily-of-the-valley (*Convallaria*) makes a sweet cut flower, but has a reputation for being difficult to establish in a garden. Look out for double-flowered *C. majalis* 'Flore Pleno' and pink-tinged *C.m.* var. *rosea*. All parts of the plant are toxic to humans and pets, so take the necessary precautions. If picking, cut when the lowest buds have started to open.

HOW? Buy potted plants in spring and plant them up in a shady spot with a good amount of leafmould in each planting hole. Once happy, the plants will spread by means of underground rhizomes.

Biochar

Biochar is charcoal used in horticulture. The benefits of it have long been known, and it was popular with South Americans centuries ago, to improve the soil, but so far Westerners have failed to exploit its potential. In the garden or on the allotment it can improve the structure of both sandy and clay soils, hold on to moisture and nutrients and gradually feed the soil. When used in a terrarium it will retain moisture, prevent root rot and absorb odours, which can build up in a very humid environment. Horticultural charcoal is much finer than other charcoal, so do not be tempted to use barbecue charcoal. Seek out locally made charcoal too. Often charcoal available for sale is the burnt remains of endangered tropical hardwoods. It is much better to use biochar from sustainably managed local woods.

Highlighting the simple beauty of a particular plant can make a striking feature. Fritillary works well in an unsealed terrarium, as does lily-of-the-valley.

Making a
sealed terrarium

What you will need

- Large plain glass container with lid
- Small pebbles
- Biochar (see page 29)
- Potting compost
- Chopsticks, to manoeuvre plants into place
- Small plants (see separate sealed- and unsealed-terrarium plant lists, box right and page 33)
- Herb clippers that are small enough to use for pruning (for general maintenance)

Sealed-terrarium plants

Look for plants that like damp, humid conditions and that can cope with low light levels.

- *Asplenium marinum*
- *Blechnum penna-marina*
- Mini hostas such as *Hosta* 'Small Parts'
- Mosses from the garden
- *Selaginella kraussiana*
- *Selaginella uncinata*
- *Trichomanes*

Preparing the container

Put a 2.5cm/1in layer of small pebbles mixed with a small amount of biochar, in the base of the jar. On top of this, add 5–7cm/2–3in potting compost. Just moisten the compost; do not soak. Lightly press down the compost.

Planting up

Using chopsticks, create a hole for each plant; insert and firm in around it. Then you can add moss from your garden or bits of twigs covered in pretty lichen, if you want. Place the lid on the container. Do not worry if condensation forms. This shows the conditions are perfect for your plants. If condensation does not occur, remove the lid and give the plants a misting; then replace the lid.

A hot, sunny
windowsill
will scorch
the plants
inside your
terrarium. A
cool, shady
windowsill
is ideal.

Unsealed terrariums
for succulents

Making an unsealed terrarium for succulents

- Create a well-drained growing mixture by mixing one part perlite with one part horticultural sand and two parts potting compost. Alternatively buy a specialist cacti compost already blended.
- Insert a layer 2.5cm/1in deep of small pebbles and then cover with potting mix, 5–7cm (2–3in) deep.
- Plant up your succulents.
- Give them a small amount of water; do not overwater.

GROWING TIPS

- Do not place in direct sunshine as the glass of the terrarium will magnify the sun's rays and cook the plants inside. Even succulents used to desert conditions will suffer.
- It is a good idea to water plants with rainwater if possible.
- Misting lightly can be the best way to introduce water into your terrarium without overwatering.

Unsealed-terrarium plants

- *Aeonium 'Kiwi'*
- *Echeveria*
- × *Graptoveria*
- × *Sedeveria*
- *Sedum*
- *Sempervivum*

Preserving jars make marvellous containers for succulents. Gather a group together to make a table centrepiece for a dinner party.

Alpine theatre

Alpines are some of the first plants I bought when I was a child, saving my pocket money for a trip to the garden centre. I think very fondly of them – there are few things as impressive as an alpine house in full flower. However alpines do have a bit of a fuddy-duddy image. Although the classic ways to grow them are in stone troughs or rock gardens, for me the tiny flowers and mounds of foliage are perfect for displaying indoors for a few weeks, when they are in their prime, before you plant them outdoors.

My inspirations for this project were the auricula theatres of Victorian Britain, which made a feature of displaying these small plants on a series of shelves or tiered staging. I wanted to bring the concept up to date as well as take ideas from vintage finds and the flea markets I love so much. For me the industrial look of this wire shelving unit was just what I was searching for. Old wooden apple crates would have worked just as well.

I thought about the containers too. I wanted to use something that carried on the industrial, pared-back theme – a container that contrasted with the delicate beauty of the alpines – so I tried tin cans, terracotta or plastic pots disguised with hessian or pretty fabrics, or sought unusual objects such as vintage cake or bread tins. As these plants need good drainage I made sure that their pots had drainage holes – and drilled some, where necessary.

Newly purchased alpines will be fine in the potting mix they are already planted in for the short duration they will be displayed indoors. However, when you come to plant them outdoors, you should give them the best growing conditions with their own special compost blend. You do not need to make their permanent home in a stone trough. Instead, try a large zinc bath and create a mini alpine garden; or plant in a green roof on your shed or even on top of your bird table roof.

OTHER IDEAS

If alpines don't take your fancy try a display of primulas, succulents or cacti.

The tiny flowers of *Saxifraga* 'Peter Pan' and *S.* 'White Pixie' look good in an alpine theatre.

Easy-going alpines

- Alpine pinks such as *Dianthus* 'Pixie', *D.* 'Whatfield Wisp'
- *Geranium cinereum*
- *Helianthemum*
- *Phlox subulata* 'Purple Beauty'
- *Saxifraga* 'Peter Pan', *S.* 'White Pixie'
- Low-growing *Sedum* such as *S. sexangulare*
- *Sempervivum*
- *Zaluzianskya ovata*

To create a neater, prettier finish when potting, add a layer of small gravel stones, to hide the potting compost.

Making an
alpine theatre

What you will need

- A tiered shelving unit or similar
- Containers with drainage holes
- Potting compost mix (see box, below right)
- Alpine plants (see page 35)
- Topdressing of grit or small pebbles

Even a few pots can make a dramatic display when placed together. You can use matching containers or else a mixture of styles in similar colours or materials. In this display I have chosen only metal planters, to keep an industrial look that blends with the wire-basket shelves.

Potting mix for alpines

Alpines need a slow release of nutrients and not the high amounts of fertilizers found in multipurpose composts. Therefore use John Innes No. 2 or No. 3 potting compost. It is now possible to buy John Innes blends that are peat-free; these help to preserve the peat bogs from further extraction. Mix together two parts potting compost, two parts leafmould, one part grit and one part horticultural sand. If you do not have leafmould, just increase the amount of compost appropriately. A good test of whether you have the right consistency is by moistening the compost mix with water and squeezing a handful in your fist. If it falls apart, that is perfect; if it forms a clump, you need to add a little more grit or sand.

Woodland display

Woodland walks through carpets of bluebells, wood anemones and wild garlic are among my favourite outings. Mossy stones, lichened branches and the gnarled bark of ancient trees fascinate me. This woodland project takes its inspiration from how tiny plants make their homes in the most unlikely of spots, appearing from the hollows of a rotten bower or in the tiniest amount of soil among the roots of a tree.

What you will need

- Hollowed-out log
- Piece of old compost bag
- Potting compost
- Home-made leafmould (optional, see page 41)
- Spring plants: sweet violets, dog violets, wood anemones, small ferns, primroses

Finding your log

Approach local tree surgeons, coppicers, woodland centres or wood recycling shops. I found the log shown opposite on a beach in Devon, where it had been washed ashore by winter storms. You could hollow out a stump of wood using a drill or chisel. Do not take logs from woodland (see Guidelines for foragers on page 15).

At spring plant fairs you will see a wide selection of woodland plants on sale.

Making a woodland display

- Work with the natural shape of your log. If you plan to stand it upright, cut a piece of old compost bag and push it into the hole to act as a makeshift container. If your log lends itself to lying on its side then this may not be necessary.
- Place your log where you want it to be displayed. Out of direct sunshine is best as these are woodland plants, which prefer dappled shade.
- Add some leafmould, if you have some, to the potting compost. Then moisten the compost mix before adding it to the log hole.
- Plant up with your woodland plants.
- Water sparingly so that you do not drown the plants.
- Once your plants have flowered, move them to a shady spot in your garden.

Sweet violets

WHY? The perfume of sweet violets (*Viola odorata*) takes me back to childhood holidays in the south-west of the UK. In fact sweet violets have been used as a fragrance since the Ancient Greeks, and they were a particular favourite of the Victorians and Edwardians. Even though they appear in woodland margins and shady hedgerows from early spring, it is easy to pass by the tiny flowers. These lovely additions to any garden make perfect tiny posies and are useful too for creating woodland-inspired projects. Many violets are available from shady-plant specialists or wildflower nurseries. For something a little different try V. 'Lianne' (which used to be a popular cut flower variety in France), *V. odorata* 'Alba' (which has crisp white flowers) or *V.o.* 'Melanie' (a floriferous variety with pink blooms).

HOW? Grow sweet violets from seed sown fresh in summer, or buy them as plants from specialist nurseries.

Wood anemones

WHY? These flowers remind me most of one of my favourite spots, an area of ancient woodland not far from my home. The white, starry flowers of wood anemones (*Anemone nemorosa*) light up the woodland floor, making the most of the sunshine streaming through the as yet leafless canopy of deciduous trees. This plant is toxic.

HOW? Plant the rhizomes in early or mid-autumn under deciduous trees and shrubs. They will particularly like a covering of leafmould or composted bark. Alternatively buy plants in spring and plant up. This is a more expensive way to grow wood anemones, but can be a more reliable way to get them to establish.

Moschatels

WHY? An unusual and hard-to-spot native is moschatel (*Adoxa moschatellina*). Its other common name, townhall clock, relates to its five flowers – four growing at right angles to each other with the fifth flower on top, facing upwards. Its green flowers add to the novelty factor of this little plant, which also emits a musky fragrance during the evening. If you are lucky you will find it thriving in the dark, damp conditions of woodlands and hedgerows, where it flowers from early to late spring. It is an intriguing plant for creating a woodland display.

HOW? Seek out a specialist nursery and buy small plants in spring. Recreate the conditions moschatel loves in the wild by incorporating leafmould into the soil, to provide a moisture-retentive environment.

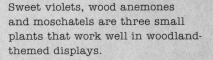

Sweet violets, wood anemones and moschatels are three small plants that work well in woodland-themed displays.

Making leafmould

Leafmould is simply composted leaves. It is what happens in nature when leaves fall to the ground and are slowly broken down over time by the weather, by creatures that live in the soil and by bacteria. Although leafmould is relatively low in nutrients, it is a fabulous conditioner, improving the structure of the soil, and it is loved by woodland plants. You will not be able to find bags of leafmould at your local garden centre, but the great news is that it is easy to make and requires very little effort on your part. Because leaves take longer to compost than other green waste, it is best to compost them separately. Fill bags with fallen leaves in autumn. You can buy hessian sacks, but I have found these break down more quickly than the leaves inside. Old compost bags work really well or you can devote a compost bin just to leaves. I use old plastic dustbins with holes punctured in the bases and sides.

The key to making good leafmould is to keep the leaves moist; they will break down much faster that way. Therefore keep an eye on them and water if necessary. After a year they will have started to break down and can be used as a mulch on your borders. If you want a finer-quality leafmould, which has turned into a rich, dark, crumbly consistency for use in pots when mixed with potting compost, you will have to wait another year.

I make my leafmould in plastic dustbins, but you could also use old compost bags or sacks with holes in them.

Twig and bark pots

I like to recycle jars and cans and choose them as simple and thrifty vases. They look great used plain but why not decorate them with foraged finds?

What you will need

- Natural materials: pieces of gnarly bark, peeled silver birch bark, dogwood stems, birch stems
- Jam jars and tin cans
- Hemp cord or similar natural thread; or PVA glue or hot-glue gun
- Rubber bands
- Spring flowers and foliage: ferns, ivy, periwinkle, primroses

Other variations for twig and bark pots include pieces of bark and leaves from ivy, bay, *Fatsia japonica* or autumn-coloured plants.

TOP TIP

If tying plant stems with hemp cord seems too difficult, then you can always use a hot-glue gun and stick them directly on to the jar or container.

Making a dogwood vase

Preparing the stems

Remove a few stems from a dogwood shrub and cut them into shorter pieces, just slightly taller than the jar. Make enough pieces to cover the whole jar. You can attach using a hot-glue gun if you want but for a more natural approach use hemp cord. Cut two lengths of hemp, each at least three times the circumference of your jar – you may need them longer depending on the thickness of the stems. Lay out both pieces of cord parallel to each other and place your first stem in the centre. The cords should be 2cm/¾in from the top and from the bottom of each stem. Take hold of the ends of one cord, bringing them over the stem and tying to secure. Repeat with the other cord.

Creating the stem sleeve

Repeat with each stem until you have reached the desired circumference for your jar. Secure each end and then tie together to form a stem sleeve to fit over your container. Trim any stems that protrude too far above the rim.

Making a silver-birch vase

- Gently peel a few pieces of the papery bark from a silver birch tree. This does not harm the tree at all. Try to keep the pieces in as large a section as possible – your technique should be a bit like trying to peel an orange in one go.
- Spread a layer of PVA glue around your jar and leave for a minute or so for the glue to become tacky. Then press pieces of the bark on to the glue. Do not worry if they reach beyond the top and bottom of the jar because these can be trimmed once the glue has dried.
- Stretch a couple of rubber bands around the jar to hold the bark in place. Lie the jar on its side and leave for a day or so. Then trim the bark if necessary, so that it is flush with both the top and bottom of the jar. It is now ready to display your spring flowers.

Tulips

WHY? Tulips (*Tulipa*) make a classic spring cut flower, and the joy of growing your own is the wealth of varieties from which you can choose. I cannot imagine my garden in spring without tulips. In fact I love them so much that I devote a bed to them on my cut flower patch. By growing them there I can pick them without feeling guilty. With so many to choose from it is hard to pick favourites, but here are a few tulips that I love: *Tulipa* 'La Belle Époque', T. 'Groenland', T. 'Verona', T. 'Antraciet' and T. 'Ballerina'.

HOW? These bulbs can be a bit temperamental, as they do not like sitting in wet soil and are prone to infections, which stunt growth and damage the flower buds before they emerge. Some varieties are less likely to return year after year. If your garden soil is predominantly clay and you live somewhere prone to wet winters you might be best treating your tulips as annuals and replant them every autumn. You could also grow tulips in raised beds or pots, where drainage is better. It is best to plant tulips later than other bulbs – wait until late autumn when the soil should be colder and hopefully your tulips will be less prone to attack from the virus tulip fire. Plant to three times the depth of the bulb with the pointed end facing upwards.

Scented narcissi

WHY? These are a must for a spring garden. Not only can you plant narcissi (*Narcissus*) direct into the garden, but they also work well in pots. If you devote a section of a cutting patch to them you can pick bunches throughout spring, to perfume your home. Certain varieties can be forced into flower much earlier too, for indoor winter blooms (see page 162). My favourites include *Narcissus* 'Silver Chimes', N. 'Avalanche' and N. 'Cragford'. All are multiheaded varieties with incredible perfume.

HOW? Narcissi are not especially fussy about their growing conditions. They prefer a sunny spot, but can tolerate a little shade. Plant the bulbs between early and late autumn, with the pointed end facing upwards and to about three times the depth of each bulb.

Columbines

WHY? No spring garden is complete without a couple of columbines (*Aquilegia*). The roots and seeds of this relative of monkshood (*Aconitum*) are poisonous, but the flowers make an attractive addition to any spring vase, where they will last about five days. The native columbine (*Aquilegia vulgaris*) with its dark purple flowers will probably make its way into most gardens of its own accord and will then happily self-sow, often sending up pink variations. Pretty as these are, there are plenty of others to squeeze into your garden too. Columbines cross-pollinate incredibly easily, which explains why there are so many different varieties to choose from. Most colours are represented, from the almost black flowers of *A.v.* var. *stellata* 'Black Barlow' to the hot colours of *A. skinneri* 'Tequila Sunrise'. Then there are the different flower forms to choose from, whether it is the tightly ruffled *A. vulgaris* var. *stellata* 'Nora Barlow' to the large, classic spurred form of *A.* 'Dove' (Songbird Series).

HOW? Columbines thrive in partial shade in a cottage-garden-style planting and will benefit from a mulch of garden compost in autumn and spring. If you are growing from seed, sow from mid-spring to early summer in seed trays. Pot on and protect from the worst of the winter weather in a cold frame or greenhouse. Plant out in spring, when you should get your first flowers. Alternatively buy mature plants from specialist nurseries.

Tulips, scented narcissi and columbines can all be used in the nature-inspired vases.

Spring
in a teacup

Afternoon tea taken outdoors in the sun, the smell of newly mown grass and the sight of daisies (*Bellis*) are all signs that spring is well and truly here. This project takes all these elements and puts them together in this cute table decoration, which would be perfect for weddings or a gathering of friends.

Growing wheat grass

Wheatgrass (*Triticum aestivum*) is popular for its supposed health-giving properties and is commonly used in juices and smoothies. If you want to grow it for those purposes, you should follow the supplier's instructions for using wheatgrass as a sprouting seed, so that it is safe to ingest. For this project however you can sow the seeds very densely, so they are touching each other on the compost surface. Cover with a fine layer of compost and then water. Place the pot somewhere warm and sunny. Germination should take only a day or so.

Making spring in a teacup

As the teacup has no drainage, make this temporary display the night before or on the morning of your event. It should look good for a few days, then you can just empty the contents on to your compost heap.

- Within 7–10 days of sowing, your wheatgrass should be at the perfect height for using in this project. Tip out the plants and compost carefully. The roots should have formed a mat and the compost should hold together. Gently pull out clumps of the grass, keeping the compost around the roots intact, and place them in your teacup.
- Cut some daisy flowers, with stalks as long as possible, and place them among the grass. You can use daisies from your garden or buy in plants of the cultivated varieties such as *B. perennis* Bellissima Rose.
- Lightly water, then keep the display somewhere cool until it is needed.

Daisies

WHY? The common daisy (*Bellis perennis*) is despised by those who crave the perfect lawn. I love them. They are the simplest of flowers, a cheery yellow disc packed with a multitude of tiny disc florets, surrounded by petal-like, white ray florets. I remember spending hours engrossed in the making of daisy chains as a child. I cannot understand why you would want to take weedkiller to these gems. I have long since abandoned the idea that weeds are purely a nuisance. Whether it is sorrel (*Oxalis*) seed pods, dandelion (*Taraxacum officinale*) flowers, roadside grasses or the common daisy, I have embraced the idea that there can be beauty in the most unlikely of places. I therefore use them all in flower arrangements. Common daisy is fairly ubiquitous, flowering from early spring if the weather is mild, so if you do not have any in your garden they are easy enough to forage. It was one of the first plants to be cultivated, and fancier versions were hugely popular with the Victorians. Varieties such as *B. perennis* 'Pomponette' are perfect for growing in containers or edging borders for spring colour.

HOW? As daisies are perennials, they should be sown in late spring or early summer so that they flower in the following year. If you forget or do not have the space to grow them from seed, they are easy to buy as plug plants in autumn and early spring, from garden centres or by mail order. When planted somewhere sunny, daisies will flower well into summer.

Swap the common daisy for the cultivated versions for an added injection of pink, or use a mixture of both types.

Press flowers

- -

Pressing is an incredibly easy method of preserving plant material and has been around for millennia. It has been a popular way to create folk art and also an essential tool for plant hunters when recording finds on their explorations. Pressed leaves and flowers have even been found in ancient burial chambers. The art of pressing plants did perhaps have quite an old-fashioned image but now that home-made gifts are all the vogue once again flower pressing is due a comeback. Because pressed flowers and leaves can be used in various ways, it is just your choice of design that determines whether they look trendy or like something from a museum collection. They work particularly well when combined with handmade papers.

Ready-made flower presses are readily available from craft shops and online, but it is not difficult to make your own. If you do buy a press, remove the corrugated card it is most likely to have arrived with because it will leave ridged indentations on your preserved specimens. Use it for something else or recycle it; then replace it with flat pieces of cardboard.

You can purchase slices of a whole range of beautiful woods from woodcraft specialists, saw mills or coppicers, who should be able to cut your chosen wood to size too. It is best to allow wood to season (dry out) for a short time before you use it as it can warp as it adjusts to the humidity of your home. If you buy from specialist wood suppliers they should have already seasoned wood available.

BELOW Cutting the corners of your cardboard and blotting paper at an angle to fit against the bolts will help to keep the sheets aligned and in place.

Making a flower press

- Place the two slices of wood together and mark with a pencil on the top plank where the hole in each of the four corners should be.
- Holding the two pieces of wood together, drill the appropriate holes and smooth any rough edges using the abrasive paper.
- Insert the bolts through the holes of the bottom slice of wood, then lay a piece of cardboard followed by a sheet of blotting paper on top.
- Place a selection of flowers and leaves on the blotting paper and then cover with another sheet of blotting paper, followed by a piece of cardboard.
- Repeat the layers of blotting paper, plants, blotting paper and cardboard several more times.
- Finally place the top slice of wood in place and secure by screwing down the wing nuts.

BELOW Space the flowers out sufficiently so that when they are pressed down they will not overlap.

TOP TIPS

- It is advisable to select flowers with a single layer of petals because they can be laid flat more easily. Thicker flowers do not work particularly well as they contain more moisture.
- Tighten the nuts on your press every week as the material inside dries out.
- Flowers should be ready to remove from the press after 2–3 weeks.
- Carefully remove your flowers from the blotting paper, using tweezers.
- Do not use kitchen paper as a substitute for proper blotting paper as the indentations on the kitchen paper will appear on your pressed flowers.

What to press

- Autumn leaves
- Ferns
- Forget-me-nots
- Geums
- Ox-eye daisies
- Poppies
- Violas

Feel free to experiment though – that is all part of the fun!

ABOVE Tighten the nuts every week to help to flatten out the drying material.

Ditch the plastic! Jute and wool-based twines and hemp cord are great compostable additions to your natural arrangements.

Natural ribbons

There is a huge amount of waste generated by the floristry industry, whether it is transparent wrapping paper or huge plastic bows. So much of it is unnecessary and detracts from the true beauty of the plant material, and there are also the obvious environmental issues. Most plastic is derived from oil – a diminishing resource, which would be better used for more essential products while we have any of it left, rather than on plastic sheets to wrap up flowers. Ditch those hideous shiny bows, which will only end up in landfill, and turn to more natural products for your arrangements. Jute and wool-based twines, hemp cord, raffia and cotton ribbon are all made from natural fibres and are therefore compostable. Or choose pretty ribbons, which you can recycle on other projects. It is even possible to buy lovely silk ribbons that have been hand-dyed using plant materials. Choose any of these to complete your projects, and they will look so much more in harmony with your home-grown flowers and foraged finds.

Summer crafts

Introduction

Of all the seasons it is summer I look forward to the most. The warmth of the sun on my skin, the fresh smell of cut grass, walks among the orchids and ox-eye daisies (*Leucanthemum vulgare*) of my local meadows, picking the first sweet peas (*Lathyrus odoratus*) and drinking in their intoxicating scent – these all sum up summer to me. The long, dark nights of winter are a distant memory as I potter in the garden until it is time for bed. There is something quite magical about a garden on a balmy summer's evening as moths flit by and bats swoop overhead. Heady aromas of honeysuckle (*Lonicera*) and night-scented stock (*Matthiola*) linger in the air. Beachcombing and wild flowers, as well as edibles from my allotment, inspire me to capture the essence of summer.

Abundance is the word that springs to mind at this time of year, and it seems a pity to resort to imported flowers when, with a little thought and planning, your own garden and allotment could provide enough natural decorating material. Having a dedicated cut flower patch or incorporating plants for this purpose in among your garden borders are ways of ensuring you have plenty of home-grown material, but you do not need to rely just on these. Colourful vegetables can make attractive and quirky table decorations; herbs are perfect for adding aromas to pretty posies; and what about trying the technique of drying and preserving summer flowers and grasses?

The sun setting on a hay meadow teeming with cowslips and orchids is a lovely scene.

Scented
arrangements

I cannot imagine my garden without scent and there can be few better things in life than the fragrance of plants mingling in the warm summer air. Here I was inspired to capture the essence of summer and create an arrangement with maximum impact using some of my favourite scented plants. This project would be perfect for a hall table or as the focal point for afternoon tea or a celebration meal with friends and family. Pick perfumed flowers and scented foliage from your garden or devote an area specifically to growing scented cut flowers.

What you will need

- Watertight, opaque container
- Coated chicken wire or the simple metal version
- Wire cutters
- Scented foliage (optional) – English mace, mint, lemon balm, scented-leaved pelargoniums
- Scented flowers – phlox, carnations, pinks, sweet Williams, stocks, freesias, honeysuckles, sweet peas, tobacco plants
- Other material of your choice to fill
- Secateurs

Preparing the container

A traditional vase will hold your blooms in place without the need for any extra help. With a wide container however you will need to give cut flowers and foliage extra support to make them easy to arrange without them flopping over. Chicken wire is great when you are using a container that you cannot see through and do not want to use florists' foam (see page 97). Cut a sheet of chicken wire that is at least twice the size of the top of your container. Take care not to scratch or cut yourself on the wire as you trim it. Mould the piece of chicken wire into a loose ball shape so that it fits snugly inside the vase. Once inserted you can adjust the shape of the wire mould so that it fits securely in place. Ideally the top of the chicken wire will sit at two thirds the height of the vase, so it provides maximum support to the plant stems without being noticeable.

Arranging the plants

Fill your container two-thirds full with tepid water. Arrange your stems of foliage and flowers into the holes in the chicken wire so it holds them in place. If the display is to be seen from all sides you want the tallest flowers in the centre, with shorter stems graduating in height down towards the front. If not, decide on a front and arrange the tallest material towards the back, graduating down towards the front. Start with stems of foliage, then add fillers, followed by your 'star' flowers. Finally add wispy stems – of a plant such as honeysuckle (*Lonicera*) or clematis.

Freesias

WHY? Freesias originate from Africa and have a spicy, peppery scent, which is quite unusual. The flowers open in succession along the length of their arching stems and add a touch of the exotic to pots, borders and flower arrangements. They grow from corms, which are similar to bulbs. If you have tried to grow freesias before but not had any luck, it could be because the corms have been stored incorrectly. Do not be tempted by those packs in supermarkets or the ones dangling from a hook in the garden centre; instead buy from a specialist bulb supplier.

HOW? Freesias can be planted directly into the ground but as they are tender you will need to wait until the soil has warmed up in late spring. Plant 3cm/1¼in deep and about 7cm/3in apart. The flower stems tend to be floppy, so a nest of twiggy pea sticks will help to provide some support. But, to get a head start, I like to plant freesias in mid-spring into pots, which I keep in my greenhouse or cold frame. Plant three or four corms, 3cm/1¼in deep, into each 1-litre pot filled with a mix of multipurpose potting compost and a little grit. For the first few weeks keep them out of direct sunlight: the bottom shelf of greenhouse staging, tucked away in the corner, is perfect as this allows the roots to become established; otherwise keep the pots in a cold frame or sheltered porch. Once they are growing, feed with liquid seaweed or comfrey fertilizer every week or so.

Phlox

WHY? Phlox comes in a variety of forms from the classic perennial border plants to the tiny alpine ones. If you are looking for another scented flower to add to your cutting patch, try growing the annual phlox *P. drummondii*, which is a native of the south-eastern United States, where it can be seen growing in drifts alongside the motorways. *Phlox drummondii* 'Grandiflora Mixed' has tall stems that are perfect for cutting, and it comes with flowers in a variety of pinks, whites and cerise.

HOW? It is easy to grow and perfect for adding to a cut flower patch. Phlox is half-hardy, so sow indoors in early spring and plant outdoors once there is little risk of frost. Pinch out the growing tips when the plants are 10–12cm/4–5in tall. Watch out for powdery mildew, which afflicts this group of plants. To avoid it, ensure that plants do not become stressed from lack of water. Incorporating garden compost into your soil before planting will help to retain moisture around the roots. Try to water only at the base of the plant to prevent splashes on the leaves, which can encourage the spores of mildew to take hold.

When you grow scented flowers and foliage you will be able to fill your home with fabulous perfumes.

English mace

WHY? This is my favourite recent discovery. The tiny, creamy flowers of English mace (*Achillea ageratum*) are similar to those of other achillea species and are exquisite. They provide an ideal backdrop to an arrangement. I would grow it just for its flowers, yet it has the most deliciously fragrant foliage too. The light menthol aroma mixed with hints of citrus is the perfect combination in the hot, still air of summer and would beautifully enhance wedding bouquets and buttonholes.

HOW? English mace is a hardy perennial so can cope with a cold winter. It grows to about 45cm/18in tall with a similar spread and needs a sunny position with well-drained soil. If your soil is predominantly clay or prone to waterlogging, try English mace in a raised bed or large container. Buy as an established plant from a specialist herb nursery.

Pinks

WHY? The cheap, plastic-wrapped bunches of scent-less florists' carnations (*Dianthus caryophyllus*) for sale in supermarkets and petrol stations have done a huge disservice to this genus of plants. Such commercially grown carnations need to be cosseted under glass but they flower over a much longer period, making them perfect for the global floral trade. Traditional pinks on the other hand are much more robust plants, but have one flush of flowers in summer. Fortunately for us gardeners, since the beginning of the twentieth century, plant breeders such as Montagu Allwood (1880–1958) have crossed both types to produce longer-flowering, hardy garden pinks, which have lost none of their tremendous fragrance. Try growing some of the more delicate, single-flowered cousins too, which insects will love: for example, *D. superbus* and the fantastically frilly *D.* 'Tatra Fragrance'. Some pinks flower on short stems, so build up a collection of suitable pretty jars and glass bottles for displaying them.

HOW? Buy as plants or small plugs in spring. You can also grow some from seed in autumn and they will flower the following spring – try *D.* × *allwoodii* 'Fragrant Village Pinks'. But, if you want the tall stems of florists' carnations as well as fabulous scent, try growing *D. caryophyllus* 'Giant Chabaud Mixed' from seed; it will flower in the first year if you sow in late winter or early spring; use a heated propagator. It has the most deliciously sweet perfume and flowers well into autumn. Although half-hardy, *D.c.* 'Giant Chabaud Mixed' may survive a mild winter; otherwise lift it and move it into a greenhouse, take cuttings or resow in late winter. All pinks and carnations will thrive in neutral to alkaline soil and require a sunny spot.

Propagating pinks

Pinks have a tendency to be short-lived and can become woody after a few years. They are incredibly easy to propagate though, so you can keep your collection going and create new plants for free. The best time to take stem cuttings is mid- to late summer.

There are different ways to do this: you can remove a short, non-flowering stem from the plant below a leaf node with a sharp, clean knife; you can hold a non-flowering stem below a leaf node and pull the top section of a stem away from the plant (below left); or you can pull off side shoots (below right), which should come away easily with a heel at each base.

Whichever method you choose, if it is not possible to find a non-flowering stem just pinch out the flower bud from your cutting. You want your cutting to root as quickly as possible, and any flower will divert energy away from this process. You should also always remove the lower leaves from each stem cutting.

All these cuttings require the same growing conditions. Place four or five cuttings around the edge of a 9cm/3½in pot filled with a 50:50 mix of multipurpose compost and grit or with seed compost. A well-drained mix will prevent the cuttings from rotting and will encourage root formation. For the same reasons it is

Pinks can become woody and a little scruffy after a few years, so propagate new plants for fresh foliage and bountiful blooms.

often recommended to place the cuttings around the edge of a porous terracotta pot. Cover the surface of the compost with grit (below), because this will help to conserve moisture. Water, label and place a clear plastic bag over the pot. As the cuttings have been separated from the parent plant, it is important to minimize any stress. A moist environment will help with this, as will keeping them away from hot sunshine. Placing the pot on a heated propagator will help to speed up rooting, but is not essential. It should take 3–4 weeks before you see roots poking out from the bottom of the pot. When you do, gently separate the new plants and plant into individual pots.

Pick of the bunch

Here are a few of my favourite pinks (*Dianthus*):

- Ivory-white D. 'Mrs Sinkins' dates back to the mid-nineteenth century and has always been considered the classic pink with a stunning fragrance. A superb modern alternative is D. Memories, bred by Whetman Pinks.
- D. 'Doris' bears semi-double flowers in candy-floss pink with darker centres and has tall stems that are perfect for cutting and arranging.
- D. 'Gran's Favourite' has white petals with berry-pink edges and centres and will flower all summer if deadheaded.

Dianthus × allwoodii 'Fragrant Village Pinks' produces hummocks of greyish blue leaves studded with stems of clove-scented flowers.

Edible dinner
decorations

✂

What you will need

- Variety of containers: preserving jars, recycled jars and tin cans
- Edible flowers: heartsease, nasturtiums, pot marigolds, rocket, chives, dill, fennel
- Beautifully coloured foliage: chard, cavolo nero, kale 'Red Russian', beetroot 'Bull's Blood', dill, fennel, nasturtiums

The idea that edible gardening need not be about the bland and boring row on row of potatoes and onions has gained considerable momentum in recent years. Beautiful French potagers and the classic British cottage garden, where edibles and ornamentals grew next to each other, have been around for hundreds of years. But as our growing space gets smaller and more of us live in urban areas the desire to grow food that looks attractive too has become increasingly popular. Not only does the food have to look good on the plate, but it also has to appear pretty while growing. A few years ago I started experimenting with attractive edibles for decorative purposes, and it is surprising just how beautiful our food can be.

This is the project in which to channel your inner Constance Spry – the doyenne of British flower arranging – who mixed edibles with flowers in her floral designs in the first half of the twentieth century. When poring over seed catalogues during the winter, select vegetables for their fabulously coloured leaves, roots and pods and add in some edible flowers and pretty herbs. Not only will they keep your kitchen supplied but you can also pinch a few items to put into vases. Use just edibles, as in this project, or mix with ornamental flowers.

LEFT Your allotment or vegetable patch can be an invaluable source of decorative cutting material if you grow attractive edibles.

Heartsease

WHY? A common European wild flower, the wild pansy (*Viola tricolor*) is more commonly referred to as heartsease, although its long history in the countryside has thrown up an array of other monikers, from love-in-idleness and come-and-cuddle-me to (my favourite) tickle-my-fancy. Heartsease is the genetic parent of the bedding violas and pansies, and its dainty little flowers have bags of charm. Its face-like flowers – generally in the three colours of purple, yellow and white – cannot fail to cheer. Not only are they very attractive lining the edges of paths or in pots but they are edible too. They do not have any distinctive flavour as such but look fabulous scattered into a salad and are perfect for decorating cakes or puddings. I love to display the tiny stems in delicate glass bottles.

HOW? Heartsease is one of the easiest plants to grow. Sow into seed trays or modules in mid-spring through to early summer, and place them in a greenhouse, cold frame or on a sunny windowsill. Prick out and pot on and then plant outdoors once the weather has started to warm up. Heartsease will grow well in containers too. Keep picking the flowers or deadheading and the plants will go on flowering all summer long.

Nasturtiums

WHY? Nasturtiums (*Tropaeolum*) are versatile plants. You can add the peppery young leaves and flowers to salads and also pickle the seeds for a home-grown alternative to capers. In addition try the flowers chopped up in fishcakes or in a herby breadcrumb topping with fish. Nasturtium flowers can last up to a week when picked, and they work well when arranged with the deep colours of dahlias and chrysanthemums, tumbling out of vases. Take a closer look at the leaves and the unusual way the stem joins the leaf in the centre; this is known botanically as peltate. They remind me of lily pads. There are varieties that form low-growing hummocks and others that send out trailing stems, up to 2.5m/8ft long, which will scramble through your borders or up and over a trellis.

HOW? Sow two or three seeds to a 9cm/3½in pot in late spring and then plant out when there is minimal chance of frost. Nasturtiums need very little care once they are growing, and they seem impervious to slugs and snails, although they can attract blackfly. If blackfly is a problem, squish them or wash off with a blast of water from a hosepipe. Once you have grown nasturtiums they are likely to self-seed, so just weed out any unwanted plants.

To make the most of your space grow climbing nasturtiums, mixed in among French or runner beans, up wigwams of coppiced hazel poles.

Chard

WHY? Chard is a stalwart of the vegetable patch or allotment. It is one of the easiest vegetables to grow, it is very versatile in the kitchen and – if that was not enough – it can be incredibly beautiful too. Swiss chard 'Bright Lights' is the most attractive and essential if you want to add a touch of ornamental beauty to a kitchen garden. A packet of it will produce plants with crinkly green or purple-red leaves and stems in deep rich reds, pinks, yellows and orange. When lit from behind, they glow like stained glass windows. Their beauty should not be confined to the kitchen and vegetable patch though; they are incredibly effective when arranged in a vase. Once picked they will last a week or so in water and look beautiful alongside other pretty edibles or when mixed with cut flowers such as dahlias, chrysanthemums, cosmos and scabious.

HOW? Sow in early spring into modules filled with multipurpose compost. Pot on into larger pots and then plant out in late spring. You will need only a few plants as they keep producing leaves as you pick. However if you sow more than you require, you will get a greater range of colours from which you can select, and you will not end up with a batch of just one colour. The young plants show the colour of the mature plant on the stems, so it is easy to weed out the ones you do not want to keep. Chard is very hardy, so will stand well over winter; once spring arrives you can crop from another flush of leaves.

Arrange chard leaves with other edible flowers in preserving jars for the perfect table decoration for a summer gathering.

Dried summer
wreath

Dried flowers are fantastic for natural crafting. One of the problems with fresh flowers – particularly in the heat and strong sunshine of summer – is that they can wilt, even when arranged in water. The need to display fresh cutting material in water can also be quite restrictive if you want to create certain projects. Dried flowers however have been preserved and so have no need for water. This means that they can be used in all sorts of decorations from posies and wreaths to headdresses and buttonholes. They are also ideal for weddings and parties because they can be made up in advance, with none of the last-minute panic of picking and arranging fresh flowers.

What you will need

- Wire cutters
- Reel wire
- Straw or raffia
- Dried flowers and grasses: foxtail brome, larkspur, poppy seed heads, feverfew
- Thin-gauge florists' stub wire
- Secateurs
- Twine, ribbon or hessian to hang

Use grasses to cover the base of your wreath and create a backdrop for a selection of dried flowers such as larkspur and seed heads such as poppies.

Making the base

Have your wire cutters and reel wire ready. Grab a handful of straw or raffia and compress it together with your hands. You want the piece, a bit like a straw sausage, to be 3–4cm/1¼–1½in thick and 15–20cm/6–8in long. Start to wrap around the straw with the reel wire. Make sure the wire is wrapped tightly as you work and that the wire wraps are about 2.5cm/1in apart.

Forming the wreath

Keep adding more straw sausages and wrapping them with the wire, to form a longer piece. Bring the two ends together to check the circumference and keep adding straw until you reach the desired size for your wreath. Remember, the bigger you make it the more plant material you will need to decorate it. When you have reached the required circumference, join the two ends together, overlapping them slightly and keep wrapping with wire. Continue one time around the whole wreath to secure it and then snip off the wire. Your wreath might look a little misshapen, so gently mould it into a circle and tuck away any loose bits of straw or trim them away.

Although wreaths are synonymous with Christmas, there is no reason why they cannot be used as charming decorations throughout the year.

Wiring in the flowers

Rather than attaching individual flowers, which would be fiddly and take up much more time, gather together small clusters or little posies of flowers, grasses and seed heads – how many will depend on the size of your wreath and the material you are using, but the posies shown had on average fourteen stems. You want your clusters to cover the wreath base but not be too big. Using the wire, wrap the stems tightly together, then trim the stems so that the posies are each about 20cm/8in long. Place each posy on to the wreath at an angle and wire into place (see opposite). Continue this process using subsequent posies to cover the stems of the previous one until your wreath is covered. If you can still see some bare patches you can poke in extra stems of grasses, seed heads or flowers. Attach a loop of twine, ribbon or hessian to the top of the wreath so that you can hang it.

Foxtail brome

WHY? There are many grasses that make great drying material but foxtail brome (*Bromus rubens*) is one of my favourites. Its dense, brush-like flower heads work well when dried as a base for summer wreaths. Pick freshly opened flowers when they are still green. These work equally well when added fresh to flower arrangements. I love annual grasses because they are such undemanding plants. They germinate readily and take up little space, forming neat clumps, so they are perfect for fitting into small spaces. I like to use them along the edges of my cut flower beds, but you could plant them in a similar way in the garden. And if you keep picking, foxtail bromes will provide you with plenty of drying and cutting material.

HOW? Sow indoors from mid-spring to early summer and plant out when the ground has warmed up. Scatter seeds on to the surface of a tray filled with seed compost or sow a pinch of seeds into individual modules. Then cover with a layer of vermiculite to keep the seeds in place but so as not to exclude too much light. Pricking out individual grasses would be incredibly time-consuming and unnecessary, and you would end up with weedy-looking plants. Instead, plant in clusters of 6–8 plants, which will fill out to form good-sized clumps. Pick the flower heads when they are still green and dry for a few days.

Larkspur

WHY? Larkspur (*Consolida*) is one of my must-have annuals. Not only does it make excellent cut flowers and produce blooms over a much longer period than its perennial close relative (*Delphinium*), but you can also dry the flower stems to use in projects or preserve the individual flowers for natural confetti. The Holy Grail for flower drying is a bloom that dries quickly and does not lose its colour – larkspur comes out on top on both counts.

HOW? They can be sown in early autumn to overwinter and will make much taller, more robust plants this way. I prefer to sow my autumn- and spring-sown larkspur into seed trays or modules and pot on. I plant them out only when they are about 10cm/4in tall and have formed stocky plants – they are much more likely to withstand any slug attack this way. Autumn-sown larkspur can grow to more than 1m/39in in height, while spring-sown ones will be about 70cm/28in. Both will benefit from staking or being grown through pea netting as it is easy for a storm to flatten them. Pick stems for drying when all the blooms have opened but the bottom flowers are still fresh.

Recommended varieties of larkspur

Consolida ajacis Giant Imperial Series produces tall, robust plants and long stems covered with flowers. Rather than the larger flower spikes of a typical larkspur, *C. regalis* 'Blue Cloud' bears ethereal masses of dainty, blue flowers, which look like butterflies. It is available in white too.

Winged everlasting

WHY? Winged everlasting (*Ammobium alatum*) is an everlasting flower with papery, star-like petals surrounding a yellow centre. It is a native of Australia, where it is an important food source for the Australian painted lady butterfly. Winged everlasting forms clumps and sends out tall, ribbed stems, similar to statice, from midsummer to the first frosts. You can pick it for fresh flower arrangements but the joy of everlasting flowers is how easy they are to preserve.

HOW? It is a perennial in its native Australia but should be treated as an annual in cool-temperate climates. Sow in mid-spring and grow under cover, planting out once there is minimal risk of frost. Winged everlasting can grow to more than 1m/39in, so it benefits from staking or being grown through pea netting. It needs to be picked when the central flower of the stem is just opening; it will continue to open as it dries.

Feverfew

WHY? Long grown in herb gardens and now used to relieve migraines, feverfew (*Tanacetum parthenium*) might not be a plant that immediately springs to mind when you are considering what to include in your garden, yet it has much to recommend it. The multi-branching stems and long-lasting, daisy-like blooms make it a useful cut flower. Feverfew is also a fabulous dried flower. It is useful when something delicate is required, and I love the meadow feel that the dried flowers conjure up. To preserve the flowers, pick several stems in a cluster, removing each with secateurs close to the base of the plant, and hang to dry for a week or so. You can then cut down the stems into smaller sections to fit your projects.

HOW? Feverfew grows best on well-drained soils and likes full sunshine. After the first flush of flowers in midsummer, cut the plant back and you will get a second show for late summer and early autumn. Feverfew tends to be short-lived, so collect seeds in late summer, sow immediately into pots, overwinter somewhere protected and you should have flowers the following summer. You will probably notice young plants popping up naturally, because feverfew can be a prolific self-seeder.

Preserve flowers such as winged everlasting and feverfew somewhere warm, dry and dark. A shed, garage or airing cupboard are all ideal spots.

Dried
floral headdress

What you will need

- Medium-gauge florists' reel wire or stub wire
- Wire cutters
- Floral tape in green or brown
- Thin-gauge florists' stub wire
- Dried flowers, grasses and seed heads: Hattie's pincushion, hare's tail, globe amaranth, larkspur
- Scissors

This home-made headdress using dried flowers will reflect your garden in all its midsummer splendour. Floral headdresses or circlets have made something of a comeback in recent years. I love the hippy, bohemian feel about them and they are perfect for weddings, festivals or summer parties. You can buy plastic versions, but they do not really capture the essence of summer and will only end up in landfill at some point. Meanwhile fresh flowers in a headdress might look gorgeous, but they are prone to wilting.

Making the base

Take your reel wire and create a circle which sits comfortably on your head or that of the person who is eventually to wear the headdress. Or else, you could do this by joining two pieces of stub wire together. You will need a couple of centimetres extra on the end of each side to create two loops to fix the headdress in place on your head. Wrap the wire in floral tape, angling the tape as you go.

Match the season

Adapt this headdress to reflect the season. Select late-summer dried flowers such as strawflowers mixed with seed heads for autumn headdresses, and in winter combine berries with long-lasting evergreens such as rosemary.

TOP TIP

It can take a little bit of time to master using floral tape. Initially it does not feel sticky at all, as the glue is activated by the warmth of your fingers. While holding the wire in one hand and the tape in the other, twist the wire so that the tape wraps around the wire. Keep pressing down the tape as you go, to make sure it sticks. When you have covered the length of wire in tape, snip it off and press to the wire to secure.

Making the flower posies

Take several pieces of your chosen plant material – a grass, a background piece such as feverfew and a focal flower – and make a small posy. Secure with thin-gauge stub wire and trim the stems. Then make more posies.

Attaching a posy to the base

Lay one of the flower posies on the prepared base and wrap it in place with floral tape.

Layering the flowers

Secure the next posy. The aim is to build up your flowers around the base using your new posy to cover the previous section of floral tape. Try to keep the plant material angled so that it faces the front.

Fitting the headdress

You can choose to decorate only a small section of the circle – or the whole headdress if you prefer. Make a small loop at each end of the wire, so the wire bends back on itself. Use these loops to secure your headdress into a circle so that it stays in place on your head.

Dried flower decorations can be made up days or even weeks in advance, so they are perfect for big events such as a wedding when time is at a premium.

Hattie's pincushion

WHY? Hattie's pincushion (*Astrantia*) has become a popular garden plant in recent years with its enchanting, pincushion-like flowers, a long flowering season and choice of stunning colours. What look like the petals are actually coloured bracts, which have a papery feel about them and surround the flowers in the centre. Papery flowers are often an indication that blooms will dry well, so I thought I would give them a try. Pleasingly, not only do they dry well but they also retain their colouring.

HOW? This perennial can be grown from seed but will take a few years to flower, so it might be better to seek out a good plant nursery where there should be a good selection of varieties from which to choose. White varieties prefer semi-shade, while pink and red ones develop their strongest colours when planted in full sun. Hattie's pincushion does not like to dry out so incorporate garden compost into the planting site and mulch in summer to retain moisture at the roots. Pick flowers when they have just fully opened.

Globe amaranth

WHY? Globe amaranth (*Gomphrena globosa*) is another 'everlasting' annual. It can be picked and used when fresh and will look good for weeks, or it can be dried. The small, rounded flower heads are actually made up of colourful leaves or bracts, which retain their colour once dried.

HOW? Being a half-hardy annual, globe amaranth is best sown in mid-spring. A heated propagator speeds up germination, but a warm, sunny windowsill is fine. Plant out once there is little danger of frost – generally in late spring to early summer. Globe amaranth takes a while to get going so do not worry if it appears to be not doing a great deal. By late summer it should have formed clumps about 60cm/2ft tall, and have produced plenty of flowers. They will keep coming well into autumn if you pick them regularly. *Gomphrena* QIS Series – QIS meaning 'Quality in Seed' – was bred especially for the cut-flower market and comes in a range of colours from pink and magenta to white and orange. You could also try *G. haageana* 'Strawberry Fields' for vibrant red flowers.

Hare's tail

WHY? Hare's tail (*Lagurus ovatus*) is a fabulously easy plant to grow and requires no special treatment to preserve. And how could you resist the soft, downy flower heads, which are crying out to be stroked and really do resemble a fluffy hare's tail? This annual makes small clumps and is perfect for lining the edge of paths or borders. You could even grow it in pots, and it takes up hardly any space on a cutting patch. You can use the flowers in fresh arrangements or preserve them by placing them in a container with no water, somewhere warm but out of direct sunlight. You can also hang them in a shed or airing cupboard. It will take only a few days for these grasses to become dry.

HOW? As hare's tail is a hardy annual, I sow two batches: one in early spring; and the other a month or so later, for a succession of flowers. Scatter seeds on the surface of a tray filled with seed compost and cover with a light sprinkling of compost or vermiculite. Prick out clumps and grow on in larger pots filled with multipurpose compost. Plant out in late spring and early summer. Being native to the southern Mediterranean, hare's tail prefers sandy, well-drained soils; if your soil is on the moist side, it will benefit from the addition of a little grit to the planting hole. Pick the flowers when they are plump and fully developed, from midsummer onwards.

Other summer-flowering plants to dry

- Lavender
- Quaking grass
- Small rose buds
- Sea lavender
- Statice
- Strawflower

Hare's tail is a fabulously versatile grass for crafting. It looks pretty when used to decorate presents or when wired into wreaths.

Floral
fascinator

If the dried floral headdress (see page 76) is not for you, why not try these charming hair decorations, which take next to no time to create? Adapt this and the dried summer wreath ideas (see page 70) to make wrist corsages, dried flower posies and buttonholes.

(see page 76) (see page 70)

What you will need

- Small dried flowers: feverfew, winged everlasting, rosebuds, *Briza maxima*, *Agrostis nebulosa*, hare's tails, strawflowers, Russian statice
- Fine-gauge florists' stub wire
- Hot-glue gun
- Hair clip
- Raffia or a pretty ribbon
- Scissors

Making a floral fascinator

- Make up a small posy of dried flowers and grasses. Secure by wrapping their stems with florists' wire.
- Glue in place on the top of a hair clip with the flower heads at the hinge end.
- Holding the clip open, tie a piece of raffia around the posy and clip, leaving a length for securing the binding later on. An extra pair of hands might help here. Wrap the posy and clip with raffia, working your way to the end of the clip, and secure using the loose piece of raffia.
- Put a dab of glue on the knot and trim any loose ends.

If the thought of wearing a hat to a wedding fills you with dread, try one of these floral fascinators.

Driftwood
planter

I find there is something very special about standing on a beach with an expanse of sea in front of me and the huge vast sky above. There is nowhere that I feel closer to nature, with clouds scudding past and a salty tang in the air. I can happily spend all day beachcombing and rock-pooling. Foraging for pretty rocks, shells and pieces of driftwood are the perfect souvenirs to take home to remind me of time spent on the coast. I love to seize the opportunity to study the local flora too, whether it is coastal plants thriving on rocky outcrops, such as sea thrift (*Armeria maritima*) and bird's foot trefoil (*Lotus corniculatus*); plants growing in specific habitats, such as sea

lavender (*Limonium*), on salt marshes; or the exotic, non-native plants, such as African blue lily (*Agapanthus*) and hottentot fig (*Carpobrotus edulis*), which thrive in generally frost-free climates.

Succulents have become a bit of a passion of mine, and I have the beginnings of a collection in the making. They remind me of holidays in Cornwall and on the Isles of Scilly, where you will find them growing in pots outdoors houses and cafes, tucked into crevices in walls and in among herbaceous perennials in garden borders. This combination of driftwood and unusual succulents captures the memories of such a summer holiday.

What you will need

- Plastic fruit punnet, margarine/butter container or yogurt pot
- Screwdriver or pencil
- Scissors
- Hot-glue gun
- Pieces of driftwood
- Crocks such as broken pieces of terracotta pot or stones or else pieces of folded newspaper
- Specialist cacti compost or a mix of multipurpose compost, horticultural sand and grit or perlite
- Succulents: *Echeveria* 'Blue Prince', *Sedum pachyphyllum* 'Nejedly', × *Sedeveria* 'Yellow Humbert', × *Graptosedum* 'Alpenglow', *Pachyphytum oviferum*
- Mulch of small pebbles, horticultural grit or sea glass

Making a driftwood planter

- If your chosen container does not have any drainage holes, make some using a screwdriver or sharp pencil. If it has a lip running around the top edge, snip this away with a pair of scissors to make attaching the driftwood easier.
- Use the hot-glue gun to stick short pieces of driftwood to the container. If you have any gaps where the container shows through add extra pieces of driftwood – this will also give your container more texture. Put to one side for a day or so, to allow the glue to cool and harden.
- Fill the base of the prepared container with crocks to cover the holes and prevent compost falling through. Fill with cacti compost or the compost mix, which will provide the good drainage relished by your succulents.
- Then plant up the container. Cover the compost with a mulch of sea glass, grit or pebbles.

OTHER IDEAS

Try using plants that love seaside conditions, such as sea thrift and Mexican fleabane (*Erigeron karvinskianus*).

TOP TIP

Look for sea glass. These are small pieces of glass that have been polished and smoothed by the sea and washed up on to beaches.

Propagating succulents

Another reason why succulents are such fantastic plants is the ease with which they can be propagated. Some succulents produce offsets. These little baby plants grow around the main plant and can be removed from the main plant with a sharp knife; in some cases you can simply pull them away (below). Offsets will often already have a few roots forming but, if they do not, leave them somewhere dry and warm for a few days so that the base of each offset callouses over. This might seem counter-intuitive if you have taken other types of plant cutting before, but it does prevent the base of the offset from rotting and will encourage it to form roots. When the offsets have calloused over, pot them up into a very well-drained mix of potting compost, horticultural sand and horticultural grit, then water and allow the pots to drain.

Some succulents such as × *Graptoveria* and echeverias can also root from leaf cuttings. This is like magic and is a great way to introduce children to botany. Certain echeverias are particularly easy to propagate in this way, but before doing it check with specialist succulent websites or nurseries to see which to try, or else experiment with the varieties you have. The succulent used here is × *Graptoveria*.

Remove some leaves from the main plant, with a gentle tug – you need to remove the whole leaf from the stem. Allow them to callous over as with the offsets (see above) and then lay the leaves on a seed tray filled with well-drained potting compost or specialist cacti

Make new succulent plants by placing leaves on to a seed tray filled with well-drained compost. Gradually roots and baby plants will form from the base of each leaf.

compost. The next stage will take a few weeks, but as the leaves start to shrivel you will see roots appearing from the base of each leaf followed by a tiny plant. Water the leaves occasionally but sparingly when you see the roots and the young plants forming. Once a good root system has developed, you can carefully separate each new plant from the old leaf. If you are at all worried about damaging the new plant by doing this, wait until the old leaf has completely withered away. Pot up in individual pots.

Succulents

Hardy varieties of succulent such as houseleeks (*Sempervivum*) can be grown outdoors in cool-temperate areas. They need well-drained soil, and while they can cope with the cold of winter they will benefit from being sheltered from persistent wet weather. Mine are all growing in pots, so in late autumn I bring them into the greenhouse or cold frame. A sheltered porch would be fine too.

I have an ever-growing collection of tender succulents, and these need protection from the cold and wet. They spend summer in my greenhouse, where they thrive in the warmth and sunshine, but I bring them indoors as winter approaches and they line my kitchen windowsill. Until the weather warms up once again, I give them only a very occasional watering – maybe once a month or every six weeks – so that they do not start to shrivel.

Succulents are generally trouble-free and are perfect for getting children interested in growing plants. They are also surprisingly versatile plants and have a rich variety of colours and forms. Discovering a specialist succulent nursery is like opening up a box of chocolates.

Hessian plant pouch

I love finding new sources of crafting and plant inspiration. It is fascinating to see how different cultures celebrate nature and the connection they have with the natural environment. For example, I am intrigued by Japanese appreciation of nature and how it inspires Japanese art, gardens and floral decoration. There is a simplicity and a pared-back approach, which is in contrast to my own love of flower-laden vases and a slightly unkempt meadow/hedgerow feel. A form of bonsai known as *kokedama* (meaning 'moss ball') is an illustration of how the Japanese use plants and nature to decorate their homes and celebrate special occasions. For this, a plant has its roots encased in a special clay soil mix, which is then covered in moss and wrapped in string. Originally *kokedama* would have been displayed on a special table, but the trend now is to suspend them, with the plants dangling – perhaps in front of a window or from a table centrepiece of branches.

When I first saw *kokedama* I thought they were enchanting. Then my grower's instinct took over and the practicalities of watering and feeding the plants and keeping the moss green made me wonder whether they were suitable for most time-strapped plant lovers. As I was still drawn to the pretty, little plant balls, I came up with an alternative. My own take on *kokedama* is meant as only a temporary decoration, and you should release them into larger containers or your garden once you have enjoyed them indoors. Use them to decorate a table for a family feast or for quirky wedding favours, with a tag instructing guests on how to plant them when they get home. Hessian plant pouches are a perfect way to gift cuttings from house plants such as spider plants (*Chlorophytum comosum*) and asparagus fern (*Asparagus setaceus*). As both the hessian and hemp cord are biodegradable, you can plant the whole parcel into a pot or the ground. It will break down gradually, and the roots will grow out through the material.

Look out for attractive foliage plants to fill your hessian pouches. Try spider plants or, for a touch of fragrance, use scented-leaved pelargoniums.

Making a hessian
plant pouch

Set these hessian pouches on a table,
perhaps as place markers for a dinner party,
or suspend them from a branch, but make
sure whatever you hang them from can take
the weight. They would also be a pretty way
to gift a baby plant to a gardening friend.

What you will need

- Scissors
- Hessian
- Hemp cord
- Needle
- John Innes No. 2 or No. 3
  soil-based potting compost
- Small plants: succulents,
  spider plants, small ivy plants,
  asparagus ferns

Cutting the hessian

Cut a piece of
hessian 18cm ×
12cm/7in × 5in
in size. You will
need to use a
section from the
edge of a hessian
sheet, which
already has a
hemmed side.
This should be
one of the sides that measures 18cm/7in
and will form the top of your parcel. The
hem will prevent any fraying and give a
neat edge to the finished parcel.

Forming a tube

Cut a piece of
hemp cord about
80cm/32in long.
Bring the short
sides of the
hessian piece
together to form
a tube or pouch,
with about
2cm/¾in of fabric
overlapping.
Using the hemp
cord, secure the roll of hessian in place
with a running stitch along the side. Stop
about 3cm/1¼in from the base.

Making the base and top of the pouch

Then turn and stitch all around the base of your tube, 3cm/1¼in from the bottom. When you have returned to the start pull the cord gently, while at the same time tucking in the spare fabric at the base inwards; it will come together like a drawstring pouch. Put a few small stitches in the base to hold it in place and then secure with some knots on the inside.

Use a second piece of cord about 40cm/16in long to stitch around the top of your hessian pouch. Leaving a cord section about 18cm/7in long, which will form part of your hanging loop, use a running stitch to work your way around the top of your pouch, close to the top edge. Stop about 2cm/¾in from the first stitch. You should now be left with two lengths of cord.

Planting up

Fill the pouch with potting compost and insert your plant. Now gently draw together the two lengths of cord. This will form a neat collar around your plant. You can then use the lengths of cord to hang your hessian parcel or tie it to secure the plant.

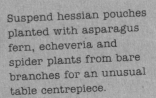

Suspend hessian pouches planted with asparagus fern, echeveria and spider plants from bare branches for an unusual table centrepiece.

Dry plants

Dried plants are perfect for crafting not only in autumn and winter but in summer too. While dried flowers will never replace fresh blooms they do have an important place in decorative arts, and can look very contemporary.

The key when using dried materials in summer projects is to pick flowers that retain their colour once dried and that conjure up that warm, sunny season. Therefore you need to select flowers that dry quickly – the best candidates are those with thin petals and single flowers. Anything that feels papery is worth trying. Also, pick seed pods when they are nicely swollen but before the seeds have ripened so that they retain their shapes.

It is also a good idea to collect plant material on a dry day, preferably from lunchtime onwards, when any dew has had a chance to evaporate.

Before you put an old flower arrangement on to the compost heap, check through it to see if any of the flowers have dried naturally. This can happen if your vase has run out of water. It is also a technique used to dry certain flowers such as hydrangeas.

TOP TIPS

- Removing the leaves is not essential; it really depends on personal preference as to whether you want to keep them. I tend to take off any foliage where it is easy to do so. Often the leaves will become dry and brittle and fall off when you come to use the dried flowers anyway.

- Bundle together small bunches – say of 8–10 stems each – and tie tightly with a piece of twine 20–30cm/8–12in long. Make a loop in the other end.

- Hang bunches somewhere warm, dry and dark – sunlight will fade the colour of your flowers and you want to preserve this for as long as possible. I use my garden shed and airing cupboard, but a garage would be fine.

- Drying time will vary depending on the plants and conditions, so you should keep checking every few days. All parts of the flowers and grasses, including their stems and any leaves, should feel dry.

- Plants respond in different ways to drying so experiment with picking and the length of time they are left to dry out.

- Once they are dry, store in boxes to keep dust-free and protected from damage until you want to use them.

- Dry more plants than you think you might need. Dried material shrinks quite a bit and can be easily damaged, and a wreath will need quite a lot of material to cover it.

Supporting cut flowers

Florists' foam was first manufactured in the 1950s. The foam absorbs water like a sponge, and stems can be pushed into the material to provide support. The foam will also gradually release water for the stems to absorb. It is popular with florists and flower arrangers as it allows them to create floral designs that would not otherwise be possible. There are drawbacks though. Florists' foam is made from a form of plastic and is not biodegradable or recyclable, and ultimately ends up in landfill. It also contains substances that some believe to be dangerous to health.

There are plenty of more natural ways to support plant material. Alternatives include pin holders and flower frogs, which sit at the bottom of your container. Some are metal or plastic discs covered in spikes; they look a bit like a pincushion covered in pins and are useful for thinner stems. Others are made from ceramic or glass and have holes, which are perfect for holding in place thicker stems, such as those of tulips or roses.

Chicken wire performs a similar support function. Cut a piece using wire cutters to fit snugly inside your container and then slot your flower stems into the holes. You can also lash a few tree branches together to create a natural grid and place it on top of a bowl or inside your container, so that it provides support for your flowers.

Autumn crafts

Introduction

As temperatures and light levels drop, nature takes on a golden hue. Woodlands which provided a lush, green backdrop to summer come into their own once more. Trees glow, being washed with reds, oranges and yellows. I love being by the coast at this time of year too. The seed heads and skeletons of cliff-top flowers and grasses silhouetted against the sky make me think of my favourite artist Angie Lewin It is the contrast between the bareness of these remnants of summer and the rich autumn colours of leaves, flowers and fruit that inspires my autumn crafting.

An early morning nip in the air and softer light heralds a move from summer to autumn. I have always loved this time of year. Perhaps strangely it feels like a new start, particularly after a lull in late summer when the garden and allotment have reached their peak and there is little more I can do. Yet in autumn I find a renewed sense of energy. There are still flowers to pick and crops to harvest as well as planning for next year, with bulbs to order and plant, and seeds to sow for an early crop of blooms next summer. And autumn is perfect too for getting out and taking inspiration from our natural surroundings. Just like squirrels storing away food for winter, now is the time to scour the hedgerows and woodland for leaves, nuts, cones, berries and seed heads – of course, leaving enough for creatures to feed on. Use some of these for projects now and store the rest to make into natural decorations for winter.

Fill boxes with pressed leaves, seed heads and grasses to use in your projects.

Hanging gardens

This is a versatile project, which could be made at any time of the year, to display whatever plant material you can find. Use the hanging jars suspended from a few branches, gathered together in a tall vase, as a centrepiece to a dinner table or hang them from chairs or door handles.

What you will need

- Wire cutters or secateurs
- 1.2mm-gauge galvanized garden wire
- Small jars – I have used old paste jars which you can find at flea markets and charity shops, but herb or spice jars would work too
- Round-nosed pliers
- Flowers and/or pretty foliage: yarrow, chrysanthemums, scabious, *Panicum* 'Frosted Explosion', heleniums, dusty millers (*Jacobaea maritima*)

① Cutting the wire for the rim

Slice off a length of wire twice the circumference of the top of your chosen jar.

② Shaping the rim wire

Place the middle of the wire against your jar and wrap it around the rim.

Making the rim loops

One-quarter and three-quarters of the way around the jar, bend a loop in the wire, using the pliers.

Securing the wire around the jar

Complete the circle around the jar by twisting the two loose ends close to the neck of the jar, then cut away any excess.

Fitting the hanging wire

Cut another length of wire that will be long enough for suspending your jar. Bend each end of the wire back on itself and hook through the loops on the wire around the jar. Fill the jar with water and a selection of flowers and foliage.

Throughout the year hang jars filled with tiny flowers in spring, sweet peas in summer and evergreen herbs and berries in autumn and winter.

Chrysanthemums

WHY? For long-lasting blooms with a choice of dazzling colours and a variety of flower forms, chrysanthemums are worthy of a spot in your garden or cutting patch. These are flowers that have suffered at the hands of the international floral trade. Pampered in glasshouses with the perfect growing conditions created by computer-controlled lighting and blackout screens, they are available year-round, encased in plastic wrapping and shoved in unattractive buckets in supermarkets or on petrol station forecourts. They, like carnations, have been done a great disservice with this 'pile it high, sell it cheap' approach. Growing your own means you can appreciate their seasonal beauty without the large carbon footprint. Depending on the variety, chrysanthemums grown outdoors will start to flower from mid- to late summer, but most come into their own in autumn. Choose varieties in deep reds, rusty oranges and golden yellows, which will perfectly match the changing season.

HOW? Buy in rooted cuttings, available from mid-spring from specialist growers. Some chrysanthemums, such as the spider varieties and those with zingy green blooms, are later into flower than others, appearing in mid- to late autumn. These are worth cultivating only if you live somewhere frost-free or if you can protect them in a greenhouse or polytunnel. If neither of these options is possible, choose early flowering varieties to make sure you get a flush of blooms before the first frost arrives. Chrysanthemums are half-hardy perennials, so in areas where frost is unlikely and where there is good drainage and a mulch covering they can survive the winter and reappear in larger clumps the following spring. If however you think your winter conditions are too cold you can treat chrysanthemums in a similar way to dahlias by lifting them before the first frost, cutting stems back to about 15cm/6in from the base and removing as much soil from the roots as possible. Put them somewhere frost-free for a week or so for the roots to dry and then pot up into seed trays or pots filled with potting compost. Keep the roots dry and frost-free over winter. Pot on in spring and start to water, planting out once there is minimal danger of frost. For new plants, take softwood cuttings from early spring growth.

Recommended varieties of chrysanthemum

Chrysanthemum 'Gompie Pink', 'Gompie Red', 'Pompom Red Bronze', 'Smokey Purple'.

Scabious

WHY? The annual scabious *Scabiosa atropurpurea* is one of the stalwarts of my cut flower patch. It is a plant that would work equally well in a garden border. Not only is it easy to grow from seed and trouble-free, but it also has a long flowering season – from midsummer to the first frosts – making it the perfect flower for beginners. Flower colours range from white, pink and deep plums to almost black, so they are versatile plants for arranging.

HOW? Sow this hardy annual in early autumn or early to mid-spring. Do this into seed trays initially and then prick out into individual modules or small pots. Plant out into the final positions from mid-spring to early summer. These scabious make quite tall plants reaching about 1.25m/4ft so will benefit from some support.

Yarrow

WHY? Yarrow (*Achillea*) is a fantastic, late-summer and autumn plant, and if you live somewhere with mild, frost-free winters it may even flower from early summer. It comes in a wide array of colours from yellows and oranges (to complement the hotter colours of other late-season plants) to beautiful, dreamy pastels. The flowers will last for a week or so when picked and arranged in a vase; they also dry well, retaining a degree of colour. Yarrow will also send out more stems as you pick during the season, although you should not expect the same level of production as from an annual flower such as cosmos. Most garden centres and nurseries will have a good selection of varieties.

HOW? It is a hardy perennial but winter wet and clay soils can be a problem, particularly for young plants. Yarrow prefers a sunny, well-drained spot and moderately fertile soil. Mulching with and incorporating some garden compost into the soil is fine, but well-rotted manure is too rich. Add grit and garden compost to heavy soils to improve the drainage. Plant and divide in spring and summer so yarrow has a chance to establish before winter. Any autumn-bought plants should be kept in a cold frame or greenhouse over winter before planting out. As with other herbaceous perennials, dividing yarrow every three years will reinvigorate the plant. You can also grow yarrow from seed, and if you sow in early autumn or from late winter to early spring it will flower in its first year.

Recommended varieties

Scabious
Scabiosa atropurpurea 'Burgundy Beau', *S.a.* 'Black Cat', *S.a.* 'Tall Crown Mix'

Yarrow
Achillea millefolium 'Cerise Queen' and *A.* Summer Berries Group can both be grown from seed; *A.* 'Terracotta' has rust-coloured flowers; and *A.* 'Moonshine' bears striking, yellow blooms.

Autumn-leaf bunting

Making autumn-leaf bunting

- Start collecting and pressing leaves as soon as they change colour and fall from the trees. Make sure they are clean and dry before you press them. Either use your flower press or put them between pages in heavy books. Leave for a week or so while they dry out.
- Take a piece of natural twine long enough to suspend in your chosen place: for example, across a mirror, window or the top of a dresser.
- Attach the leaves by tying a knot in the cord and catching the stem of the leaf before you pull the knot tight.
- Work your way along the garland, evenly spacing your leaves.
- Create loops at either end of the garland so that you can hang it up.

Nothing says autumn more than the changing colour of leaves. Autumnal leaves are fantastic for crafting as they offer lots of potential. Include them as card or present decorations, and store them for use as Christmas decorations too. To make the most of the beautiful colours, suspend your garland by a window for a stained-glass effect. Forage in a local park or woods, but do not forget the trees, shrubs and climbers in your garden. Native trees such as beech (*Fagus*), oak (*Quercus*) and birch (*Betula*) all shed beautifully coloured leaves, while there are plenty of other plants that will fit in even the smallest of gardens. Now is the perfect season, while the ground is still warm, to plant trees and shrubs, so take a trip to an arboretum or specialist nursery for inspiration and acquire some of your own autumn hues.

TOP TIP

You can adopt this technique to make all manner of garlands. Try tiny, dried hydrangea heads (as shown here) or glistening honesty (*Lunaria*) seed pods (see page 141).

Maple

WHY? The classic tree of Japanese gardens, maple (*Acer*) produces some of the best autumn-coloured leaves with delicate shapes perfect for crafting. Use them in wreaths, to decorate presents and cards or in a garland such as the Autumn-leaf bunting (see page 106). Maples are also a useful choice for gardens generally, being slow-growing, small trees. There are numerous varieties so visit a specialist nursery in autumn to see these plants at their best and to gain inspiration.

HOW? They do best in a sheltered spot away from cold winds, which can scorch leaves. Maples can be prone to pests, such as scale insect, which will try to colonize your tree in spring. Look out for hard scales on the bark and branches of the tree where the insect sucks sap from the plant, thereby weakening it. If you discover these hard scales, remove with an old toothbrush and soapy water.

Liquidambar

WHY? This is one of the few trees that can rival maple for autumn colour. Its palm-shaped leaves, which are like those of maple only less delicate, are one of the first to change colour in late summer – you may notice red tints forming before you are ready to accept that autumn is on the way. Watch as its leaves turn from a mid-green to a variety of yellows, reds, oranges and deepest cranberry. Its tolerance of pollution makes liquidambar perfect for urban gardens. *Liquidambar styraciflua* 'Worplesdon' is a popular variety with early colour. For small gardens try *L.s.* 'Gum Ball', a dense compact plant, which can be bought already grafted on to a tall, straight stem to form a lollipop shape.

HOW? Liquidambar can grow up to 25m/82ft, which is much too big for an average garden, but it responds well to pruning and I have

Recommended varieties of maple

Acer palmatum 'Osakazuki', *A.p.* 'Bloodgood' and *A.p.* 'Sango-kaku'.

seen it kept to a more manageable 10m (33ft). For the best colour grow it in a sunny spot. The pH level of your soil can also affect the strength of colour. The deepest hues occur on acid soils. Do not worry too much about this; you will still have attractive autumn colours if your soil is alkaline. However you can apply sulphur in the form of powder or chips if you would like to acidify the soil around your tree roots, to improve autumn colour – do a pH test to check first if this is necessary.

Blueberries

WHY? It might seem odd to include a blueberry (*Vaccinum*) here, yet they are not only very productive when laden with delicious fruits from midsummer but are also autumnal stunners. The leaves turn from mid-green to a deep rich red, which deepens until they fall from the plant. The small leaves are perfect for projects too. Thus blueberry plants are a surprising source of crafting material. Try the following blueberry cultivars: 'Bluecrop', 'Brigitta' and 'Patriot'.

HOW? Some blueberries are self-fertile so you can grow only one plant, but most will crop more heavily if you have another variety close by. Blueberries need to be grown in acid soils or in ericaceous compost. Unlike many other fruits, they do well when grown in containers. You will need a pot at least 30cm/12in in diameter, but the larger the better. For the best autumn colour and the sweetest fruits, plant in full sun. Water with rainwater, as tap water will raise the pH of the compost. Feed with a specialist ericaceous fertilizer – or composted pine needles, if you can get hold of them. Blueberries are generally pest-free, and birds eating your fruit will be the biggest problem. Therefore net your bushes before the fruits start to ripen, as blackbirds will strip a plant in a day.

Blueberries are a surprising source of autumnal colour. You can use their vibrant leaves then – and in winter – for crafting projects.

Winter-squash
vases

What you will need

- Selection of winter squashes
- Sharp knife
- Spoon or ice-cream scoop
- Vibrant autumn flowers: dahlias, black-eyed Susans, heleniums, zinnias, chrysanthemums

The autumn harvest would not be the same without squashes such as pumpkins. Not only are they tasty and store well into winter but they are also attractive and make a pretty display in themselves. A collection of different sizes, colours and textures in your kitchen, or as a centrepiece on your dining table, is one of the simplest ways to celebrate the season, but you can take this a step further by using some squashes as vases and by combining them with the jewel-like colours of dahlias. You will need to use pumpkins or other winter squashes, which have thick, tough skins, rather than summer squashes such as patty pans with their thinner outer layers.

Making a winter-squash vase

- Carefully remove the top of the squash using the knife. Do not cut off too much – you still want to have the curve of the pumpkin at the top so that it acts as a support for your flowers.
- Scoop out a recess inside the squash.
- Fill with water and arrange a selection of autumnal flowers.
- Although your squash should be watertight, it will absorb the water so top up every day.

TOP TIP

The squashes are best prepared the day you want your display to look at its best. If you prefer to make them the night before, store the squash vases in your refrigerator overnight.

Dahlias

WHY? Dahlias are one of the best-value plants you can grow. A small patch of dahlias will supply you with buckets of flowers from midsummer onwards, and if you are lucky to experience no frost you will still have flowers to pick right up until winter. There is a mind-boggling variety of colours and flower forms to choose from, but not all dahlias last well once cut. The Karma varieties have been bred specifically so that they have longer-lasting flowers and long stems, making them perfect for cutting, yet it is worth experimenting if other dahlias take your fancy. And the joy of growing your own is that if the flowers last only a few days there will be plenty more waiting to be picked. I love *Dahlia* 'Karma Fuchsiana', *D.* 'Karma Naomi' and *D.* 'Karma Fiesta'.

HOW? Dahlia tubers can be bought in early spring. You will find them in garden centres, but for the best choice go to a specialist grower. They start off as unpromisingly wizened tubers, like an elongated potato. Dahlias are tender and should not be planted outdoors until the ground has warmed up and frost is no longer likely. To get early flowers it is a good idea to start them off in pots in mid-spring and keep them in a greenhouse or cold frame. I have even had dahlias on my windowsills. Plant one tuber into a 20cm/8in pot filled with multipurpose compost, water lightly and keep frost-free. To prevent the tuber from rotting, keep the compost on

the dry side until you start to see growth appearing. Plant out in late spring or early summer. To get the most from your dahlias, plant them into soil enriched with compost – garden compost is perfect but shop-bought is fine too. Add comfrey pellets or comfrey leaves to the planting hole before inserting the dahlia plant. Comfrey provides the nutrients needed for flowering and will give your dahlias an extra boost. Water and protect from slugs. Once your dahlias are flowering they will benefit from a weekly feed of comfrey fertilizer or tomato food. If you live somewhere not prone to frosts you can leave dahlias in the ground to overwinter. They will benefit from a covering of compost or straw to give a little extra protection. If your garden experiences temperatures below 0°C/32°F or is susceptible to wet winters or waterlogged soil, then it is best to lift dahlias. After the first frost has blackened the plant, carefully dig them up with a fork. Start further away from the plant than you would imagine so that you do not spear any tubers in the process. Cut off the top growth about 5cm/2in from the bases and remove as much soil as possible from around the tubers. Store in a shed or garage upside down to allow the dahlias to dry out. After about three weeks, wrap them in newspaper and store in trays somewhere dry and frost-free, or else plant into dry compost. You can then replant the following spring.

Dahlias are enjoying a bit of a renaissance. Once thought of as old-fashioned, they are now deemed to be an essential bloom for any cut flower patch.

Black-eyed Susans

WHY? Rudbeckias can be annuals or perennials and have been made popular by the 'new perennial' style of prairie planting using large drifts of flowers mixed with grasses – as championed by the Dutch garden designer Piet Oudolf. For fabulous late-season cut flowers it is hard to beat the varieties of black-eyed Susan (*Rudbeckia hirta*). The colours of burnt-umber, deep reds, rich oranges and gold are perfect for autumnal arrangements such as squash vases, and the flowers can last up to two weeks once picked. Arrange with rich-coloured dahlias, grasses and seed heads such as teasels to capture the season.

HOW? Sow seeds of black-eyed Susan in mid-spring indoors and then plant out when there is little danger of frost. Plants will sulk if the weather is cold and wet, so do not be in a hurry to put them out if conditions are not right; instead pot up into a bigger pot or cover them with horticultural fleece until the weather gets warmer. You can also buy black-eyed Susan as plug plants by mail order or from a garden centre in spring, although the choice of varieties will not be so extensive. Black-eyed Susans will start to flower from mid- or late summer and continue, if you keep picking them, until the first frosts.

Heleniums

WHY? This is one of the few cut-and-come-again perennials and is another plant popular in prairie schemes. If you choose your varieties carefully, you can have flowers from midsummer. After being deadheaded or picked for a vase, heleniums will produce more flower buds right through to the first frosts. I have found *Helenium* 'Sahin's Early Flowerer' to be an incredibly robust plant, doing what it says – that is, flowering several weeks earlier than other varieties. It has dazzling, orange flowers streaked with darker oranges and reds surrounding dark brown central cones. It can grow to 1.25m/4ft tall, but does not need staking unless your site is particularly windy. Also try *H.* 'El Dorado' for its eye-catching, yellow blooms. For me helenium is the perfect autumnal flower and combines well with dahlias, chrysanthemums and black-eyed Susans to provide a last gasp of colour from the garden before winter sets in.

HOW? Helenium needs full sun and moisture-retentive soil. Divide clumps every three or four years to reinvigorate the plant, planting up the vigorous outer parts of the plant and discarding the tired central bit. Wait until spring to do this.

Recommended varieties of black-eyed Susan

Rudbeckia hirta 'Marmalade', R.h. 'Cherry Brandy', R.h. 'Chim Chiminee'

Gourds and winter squashes

Gourds are distinguished by their hard outer skins. The intriguing fruits come in a range of colours with fantastically patterned and warty varieties. Some of them can be eaten when young but most have bitter flesh so check the seed packet if you want edible fruits. Gourds however are often chosen for decorative purposes and have been for centuries. In various cultures across the world, gourds have also been used as utensils and musical instruments, while the Chinese moulded gourds to create intricately patterned bottles and containers. You can even carve the variety 'Birdhouse' to be just that – a nesting box for the birds in your garden. At this time of year you will find gourds in florist shops, but why not grow your own?

Winter squashes are grown mainly for their edible qualities, but they make attractive decorations in their own right. Farmers' markets in autumn can be a great places to source winter squashes to see which ones are the tastiest. My own favourites are the orange-skinned 'Uchiki Kuri' (also known as the onion squash), 'Crown Prince' (for its grey-blue fruit) and 'Kabocha' (dark green).

Grow gourds and the smaller varieties of squashes up trellis panels or hazel wigwams.

How to grow gourds and winter squashes

- Provide gourds and winter squashes with rich soil and a warm, sheltered site. They can take up a lot of space, so grow them up a trellis panel, a coppiced hazel framework or over an arbour. Some varieties of winter squash produce much bigger fruit than gourds and should be allowed to trail across the ground because the weight of the fruit can be too much for the plant to support.
- Sow in late spring indoors, with two seeds in each 9cm/3½in pot. Pull out one of the seedlings if both germinate.
- Plant out in early summer. Add some extra compost to the planting hole – the more the better.
- Water regularly and feed once a week with comfrey fertilizer once the flowers have started to appear.
- Harvest your fruits in autumn when their skins feel firm and the colours have developed fully.
- If frost is forecast, pick any fruit and put it on a sunny windowsill for the skin to mature.
- If you want to eat your winter squashes it is important to 'cure' the fruits immediately after harvesting, which improves their ability to be stored and helps develop their flavour. To do this, give them a couple of weeks in a sunny room while the skins harden. Then store them somewhere cool but frost-free until you want to eat them.

Everlasting-
flower wreath

Although wreaths are most commonly associated with Christmas, when they adorn doors throughout the festive period, they are such versatile decorations that they should not be restricted to just a couple of weeks in winter. This wreath has a straw base like my one for the dried summer wreath (see page 70), but you could also weave together hazel branches or bendy birch twigs. Then it is just a case of gathering together the material you want for decoration. Autumn provides so much to choose from, and in this project I have chosen a mass of strawflowers (*Xerochrysum bracteatum*) for a splash of seasonal colour. This is not a weatherproof decoration so hang it indoors or on a sheltered door.

What you will need

- Wire cutters or secateurs
- Reel wire
- Straw or raffia
- Thin- and medium-gauge florists' stub wire
- Grasses, seed heads and dried flowers: strawflowers, poppy seed heads, love-in-a-mist, shoo-fly lanterns, hops
- Ribbon, hessian or twine

Making an everlasting-flower wreath

- Create the base as for a Dried summer wreath (see page 70). Vary the size if you want, but take into consideration how much material you have available for decoration.
- Gather together three or four stems of strawflowers and wire tightly together with thin-gauge stub wire, to create a small posy – just like the posies for the dried summer wreath. Trim the stems so the posy is about 9cm/3½in long. Make up all your posies – this wreath needed nineteen posies to cover it completely.
- Place a posy on to the wreath base and wire into place with medium-gauge stub wire. Using subsequent posies to cover up the wire of the previous posy, work your way around the wreath until it is completely covered. Make sure you place your posies tightly together so that the final wreath does not have any gaps. If there are any small holes, poke in some extra flowers.
- Use ribbon, hessian or twine to hang your wreath somewhere sheltered.

Use posies of love-in-a-mist or poppy seed heads as an alternative to strawflowers to cover your wreath base.

Strawflower

WHY? There is a certain kitschness about brightly coloured strawflowers (*Xerochrysum bracteatum*), which I love. Sometimes there are plants that I might not want to include in my garden because they do not fit with the style of planting, yet they have qualities that make me still want to grow them; I would include strawflowers in this category. A small patch tucked away on an allotment or cut flower patch is perfect for this type of plant. The papery flowers of this 'everlasting' plant can be enjoyed when freshly picked. Alternatively dry them for a week or so, to preserve their fabulously vibrant colours for use through autumn and even winter.

HOW? Sow seeds indoors about two months before you would expect to have your last frost. Prick out and pot on until it is warm enough for the strawflowers to be planted outdoors. They should flower from midsummer into autumn. They grow to about 1m/39in tall, so support from canes and twine or netting is helpful. Pick when the first few layers of petals have opened but the centres are still tightly closed as they will continue to open during the drying process.

Shoo-fly

WHY? Shoo-fly (*Nicandra physalodes*), a native of Peru, is similar to Chinese lanterns (*Physalis alkekengi*) in that it produces bell-shaped flowers, which develop into lantern-shaped seed pods. You can use the freshly picked stems of green or black seed pods mixed with cut flowers, or else dry the picked stems so the lanterns turn a pretty golden colour. As the name shoo-fly might suggest, this plant reputedly has pest-control properties, keeping whitefly away from your plants, so a few shoo-flies in among your cabbage and kale might be worth a try.

HOW? Being an annual, shoo-fly germinates easily from a sowing in mid-spring and should be planted out when there is little danger of frost. It is a strong grower and can reach more than 1m/39in tall, so will benefit from support.

Hops

WHY? Swags of dried hops (*Humulus*) have long been a popular decoration in country pubs and farmhouses. As well as being grown to flavour beer, hops placed in or near your bed in sachets are also reputed to aid sleep. I love them for their decorative characteristics. Drying long lengths of hop bines (vines) and then weaving them into garlands is the classic way to use them, but you can also add shorter stems or the individual flowers (the hops) to wreaths or to decorate presents. Initially the hops are a lovely pale green colour, but they will gradually fade to a golden hue. As they dry hops do tend to become brittle so need care when handled.

HOW? Hops are twining climbers often found sprawling over hedgerows. Such hops grow at an incredible rate and are much too vigorous for a garden. The dwarf variety *H. lupulus*
'Golden Tassels' however reaches a maximum of 4.5m/15ft in a season and has beautifully ornamental, golden yellow foliage. Being an herbaceous climber, it will need something to scramble up; then all of its growth will die back in autumn before starting again the following year. A trellis panel on a fence or shed wall would be perfect. Autumn and spring are the times to plant this perennial. It is important to buy virus-free plants, so purchase from a specialist grower. Hops like a sunny, sheltered site. Shoots will appear from the base of the plant in mid-spring and flowers will start to form from mid- to late summer. Harvest when the flowers have fully developed but are still tightly closed. Dry them in a warm place out of direct light. Take care when handling them because the stems are covered in tiny barbs that irritate skin.

Scour seed and plant catalogues for plants that could make great crafting material. Look out for everlasting flowers, unusual seed heads, attractive berries and stunning autumnal colour.

Picture-frame
wreath

What you will need

- Straight, pretty stems: dogwood, birch, willow
- Secateurs
- Medium- and thin-gauge stub wire
- Twine or natural cord, such as brown hemp
- Material for decorations: love-in-a-mist or opium poppy seed pods, *Scabiosa stellata*
- Ribbon, twine or raffia, for hanging the wreath

Most wreaths are round in shape but there is nothing stopping you creating one that is square, rectangular or diamond shaped, for something a little bit different. This is one of simplest and quickest designs and could be adapted throughout the year, incorporating whatever plant decorations are looking at their best.

Preparing each frame side

Cut stems into sections 35cm/14in long. You can vary this if you would like a smaller or larger wreath. Gather together a handful of stems for each side – the exact number depends on the width of the stems. I have used three per side here. With the medium-gauge stub wire, wrap the wire tightly about 6cm/2½in from each end of the stem bundle. Repeat this with the three other sides of the frame.

Joining each frame side

Take two stem bundles and hold them together at right angles, to form one corner of your wreath. Leave several centimetres sticking out on each end and then secure in place by wrapping tightly with wire. Using the hemp cord, wrap around the corner, criss-crossing from side to side and from back to front, to make sure the corners are rigid and to hide the wire. Repeat with the other two stem bundles and then join together to form your four-sided wreath.

Adding the decorations

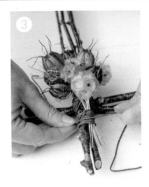

Create little ornamental posies by wrapping several stems together with thin-gauge stub wire. Attach the individual posies to the wreath with hemp cord, again criss-crossing to secure them tightly in place. Tie off at the back. You can use the posies to cover any exposed wire on the base of your wreath.

Use natural twine to attach your posies to your wreath. Flax, jute and hemp will all work in harmony with your seed heads and branches.

Opium poppies

WHY? Opium poppies (*Papaver somniferum*) are one of my favourite flowers, but in the garden and as cut flowers they are ephemeral so do not make great crafting material. Although the flowers are attractive when pressed, it is the sculptural beauty of the glaucous seed pods which makes them so invaluable. Add these to your floral arrangements when picked fresh and also cut and dry them for decorations from summer right through to winter. Opium poppies are toxic, although the ripe seeds are harmless. It is therefore best to wear gloves when handling them, and dry them out of reach of children and pets.

HOW? Sow directly into the soil from mid-spring to early summer for a succession of flowers and seed pods. Scatter in patches or sow into rows and lightly rake over with soil. You can also sow into modules and plant out in small clumps. Try to pick when the pods have swollen but before the seeds have ripened. A couple of days to a week after the petals have fallen is normally a good time. Put them head first into a paper bag in case the pods have ripened, as they produce an incredible amount of seeds and will shed them all over your drying area. Tie a piece of twine around the neck of the bag and then hang it up. Opium poppy seed pods take 7–10 days to dry. Once you have these pretty flowers they will pop up every year. If they become a nuisance they are easy to remove.

Recommended varieties of opium poppy

There are numerous varieties, from the single-flowered blooms of *Papaver somniferum* 'Cherry Glow' to the over-the-top, peony-like flowers of *P.s.* 'Black Peony'. Take your pick!

You can enjoy seed pods picked fresh and arranged with flowers or else you could dry them and store them for inclusion in your natural crafting projects.

Love-in-a-mist

WHY? Love-in-a-mist (*Nigella*) is such an intriguing flower that I would not be without it. Not only are the flowers fascinating in their complexity but they also produce the most amazing seed pods, like stripy balloons. These seed pods are fabulous when used fresh (mixed with flowers) or dried for summer, autumn and winter decorations. For the best seed pods grow *N. damascena* 'Albion Black Pod', which develops the most amazing plum colour. The flowers of love-in-a-mist can also be dried, if you pick them just as the petals start to open. Although the flowers do not retain much shape, they add a splash of colour to a dried flower project, provided you are growing the blue or pink forms.

HOW? If you want flowers throughout the summer just scatter seeds every three weeks or so from late spring in patches of your garden or on your cut flower patch. This is one of the few plants I do not start off indoors. It does not like root disturbance, but you can try growing it in modules if you do not allow the plants to become pot-bound. Pick when the pods are still fresh and the seed inside has yet to ripen – a few days after the petals have fallen is the best time. Dry both the pods and flowers somewhere dark and warm for a week or so.

Scabiosa stellata

WHY? *Scabiosa stellata* produces pretty, pale lilac flowers from midsummer until early autumn, which are loved by bees and hoverflies, but they are fleeting. It is therefore for the most spectacular seed heads that I grow this plant. Its globular pods, with their look and feel of parchment, are divided into individual sections each with a dark purple star in the centre. In fact it is hard to believe they are real. They look like nature's very own Christmas bauble. They are such versatile decorations – use them with fresh or dried flowers in summer, with autumnal leaves and berries, or store them for winter ornamentations. Among the attractive varieties you will come across are S.s. 'Stern Kugel' and S.s. 'Ping Pong'.

HOW? Sow in mid- and late spring indoors into seed trays and then plant outdoors once the danger of frost has passed. Germination can be a bit haphazard, but it is worth persevering with more sowings. The young seedlings are prone to damping off, so try not to overwater. If you keep picking the seed heads, the plants will send out new flowers. Although the seed heads do not really need any extra treatment to preserve them, I dry them for a day or so in my shed or airing cupboard.

Whimsical makes

Sometimes there does not have to be a point to making something. Simply spending an absorbing hour or two on a project can be just what you need. The little whimsical ideas shown here were initially inspired by a day beachcombing and playing in the sand with the bits and pieces I had found. At home with my glue gun and crafting toolbox at the ready, my shell flowers and butterfly as well as my dragonfly of driftwood, shells and sycamore (*Acer pseudoplatanus*) seeds came together. I had no idea what I would do with them afterwards, but at the time that was not the point. Since then I have used them to decorate presents and attached them to a band of hessian to create unique napkin holders. They would also work in transforming a jam jar into a pretty vase or pencil pot for a desk. All you need to do is keep a box of interesting natural finds – seeds, shells, feathers – that catch your eye and then get creative. These are examples of what I have made, but see where your imagination takes you.

Keep a collection of foraged finds such as shells, sea glass, driftwood and feathers and then exploit them in a variety of interesting ways.

What you will need

- Mussel shells
- Hot-glue gun
- Prettily coloured shells – in this case periwinkles
- Scissors
- Thin pieces of dried seaweed stems, driftwood or tree twigs
- Sycamore seed pods
- Brown hemp cord
- Swirly topshells

Preparing the flower

Use the mussel shells to create the petals. Join five together with glue, and then stick a coloured shell in the centre.

Making the butterfly

Replicate nature by choosing two slightly larger mussel shells for the top wings and two smaller shells for the bottom wings. For the body and antennae of the butterfly, I found this perfect thin piece of preserved seaweed stem, which had forked into two sections. Twigs are a good alternative.

Creating the dragonfly

I cut a piece of dried seaweed stem for the body. To the top of this I glued two sycamore seed pods, to make the wings. I then wrapped the hemp cord around the centre of the wings and body to form the fatter body part of the dragonfly. Finally I glued on two swirly topshells, to make the large eyes.

Saving seeds

We gardeners are a thrifty bunch – we like anything that is for free and what better way to get something for nothing than collecting your own seeds. There is also something about saving your own seeds that makes you feel like a proper gardener. I like to grow new varieties every year so need to buy in those seeds, but it is also good to have a free supply of some of my most favourite plants for sowing in spring. And if you put home-saved seeds into pretty envelopes they can make lovely presents. Autumn is the perfect time to wander around the garden and collect seed heads and pods. Although seed-saving is pretty straightforward, there are a few things to bear in mind.

AMONG THE BEST

The easiest seeds to save from your garden and cut flower patch include: briza, cornflowers (*Centaurea cyanus*), cosmos, feverfew, honesty, love-in-a-mist, poppies, pot marigolds

By attaching a pretty seed head to your seed packets you can transform them into attractive gifts for gardening friends.

TOP TIPS

- Plants grown from home-saved seed, as opposed to bought seed, will be more able to cope with your specific growing conditions.

- Do not collect seeds from F1 hybrid plants as the special characteristics of these plants will be lost in the next generation.

- Seeds may not always produce plants that are identical to the parent plant.

- Gather seeds on a dry day from mid-afternoon to early evening so that any dew has had a chance to evaporate.

- Cut stems and, while still in the garden, pop them head first into separate paper bags. If you are worried that you may not remember what stem is what, then take a pen with you and write on the bag.

- Sorting your seeds on a white surface is helpful as the seeds stand out more clearly. If you do not have a white table, a few sheets of white paper are just as effective.

- Remove the seeds from their various pods. Some seeds are very clean, such as poppies (*Papaver*), while others will come with the remnants of their protective casings, which should be cleaned off as much as possible to prevent the seeds from becoming damp. Many seeds can be picked out from the plant debris or chaff but some require a little more effort. A garden sieve or riddle can be invaluable. Another technique is to place the seeds into a bowl, shake the bowl from side to side and the bigger bits will move to the surface; you can then pick these out and the seeds should be left behind.

- Store your seeds in small paper bags or envelopes in a dry, cool place, having noted the name of the plant and the date its seed was gathered. If you want to give seeds as a gift, decorate the packaging with a small seed head from the actual plant.

Preserve plants with glycerine

What you will need

- Plant material for preserving
- Secateurs
- Deep buckets
- Glycerine
- Old glass jar
- Spoon or other stirring implement

By preserving plant material I can hold on to my garden for as long as possible. As the weather turns stormy, and wind and rain whip through the garden and countryside, plants will start to look dishevelled. It is important to get to your favourite plants early so you can preserve them at their peak. Drying and pressing are two ways of saving plant material. Another technique, using glycerine, retains the soft, supple nature of living plants.

Sourcing your material

Cut your chosen plant material and condition by trimming the stems at a sharp angle and placing in buckets filled with cool water. Leave them somewhere shady for at least a few hours – overnight is better.

Using glycerine

Mix one part glycerine with two parts hot water in an old glass jar and stir until the glycerine has dissolved. Stand to one side and allow to cool. Re-trim the stems of your plant material at a sharp angle, and then place into the jars of cooled glycerine. Stand them somewhere shady. Check them every day or so to watch their progress. Depending on your plant material and the time of year, the process can take a few days to a few weeks. When the stems are ready, remove, dry the bases and store or use immediately.

TOP TIPS

- Hydrangeas and ivy will need only a few days to absorb the glycerine, beech needs a week or so and oak can take ten days to be ready. It takes a bit of trial and error to know when your stems are fully saturated. If you leave them too long, they can wilt and you might see blobs of glycerine on the leaves. The best way to check is to feel the foliage as it will become soft and supple. It is better to under-do the glycerine process than to soak plants in it for too long.

- The technique of glycerining generally changes the colour of the leaves or material you are preserving. Although ivy will stay green it will darken in colour. It is therefore best to use plain ivy, as variegated versions will change to a muddy colour where they have white patches. Beech, if picked in late summer, will develop dark olive-green leaves and the branches will retain the outer casing of the nut with the nuts inside. These branches look fabulous in autumn and winter wreaths. If picked later, the nut cases will have fallen from the branches. Oak leaves, in glycerine, turn to dark brown.

WHEN TO PICK

Late summer is the best time to pick tree branches, because plants slow down their uptake of water as autumn approaches. The process will still work later on into autumn, but it will take a little longer as plants will not absorb the glycerine as quickly. Evergreens can be gathered into winter.

THEME:

Endangered moss

Moss is a staple of the floristry trade, where it is used to wrap flowers to retain moisture, to form a base for a wreath and to hide the construction of floral designs. It is easy to dismiss moss as just moss and not really consider it as a plant or think about its origin, but in its natural habitat it is part of a rich biodiversity of plants – just like wild flowers and ancient trees. Walk through woodland and take a closer look at what makes the scene so lush and verdant. The moss-covered tree stumps, fallen branches and stones, which cover the woodland floor, create a scene of simple beauty we take for granted. Now imagine it without the moss, and how different it would be. In parts of north-west America, moss has been over-harvested and areas still show signs of damage years later, where moss has failed to regrow.

Research has been carried out in America and Scotland to see which mosses grow back most quickly and in what quantities it can be taken, and Scottish Natural Heritage now produce a code of conduct on the sustainable harvest of moss (www. forestharvest.org.uk/guidelines/mosscode.htm). Yet, trying to find out where the moss available online or used by florists has been sourced and whether it has been done sustainably and with care for the environment are difficult, if not impossible, challenges. Fortunately most of us have damp, shady areas in our gardens where moss collects, or a moss-infested patch of lawn. Instead of seeing this as a nuisance, use such moss for your crafting projects.

TOP TIP

As well as sourcing home-grown moss, you could introduce other, alternative wreath bases of straw and raffia or instead make wreaths from willow (*Salix*), hazel (*Corylus*) and birch (*Betula*) and wire in dried material for decoration.

Winter crafts

Introduction

The run-up to Christmas can be a hectic time, but there can still be an opportunity to squeeze in a spot of crafting. Keep your ideas simple and involve the rest of the family. Not only will you have beautiful, unique decorations but you will also have created some fantastic memories. Having your own winter-crafting projects in mind will give you an excuse to get outdoors and get some much needed fresh air and exercise. Combine a Sunday afternoon walk with a spot of foraging for cones, nuts and pretty berries. Early winter storms will often bring down branches, which provide rich pickings. Add these to the goodies stored back in autumn and the surprising number of plants that are at their best at this time of year.

I have a love–hate relationship with winter. I still get excited by the festivities that mark this time of year; I could stare for hours at the flickering flames of our wood fire; and there are cosy jumpers and steaming hot stews, spicy fruit puddings, damson gin to sip on a cold, dark night and frost-edged plants glistening in the low winter sun. But I will admit I find the short days and lack of light difficult. Crafting and finding projects to keep me busy and to distract me have been my ways of dealing with the winter blues.

While I am all for a bit of glitter it is easy to overdo the tinsel and the mass-manufactured

Collect evergreens, colourful stems, berries, cones and sprigs of old man's beard for winter decorating and crafting.

decorations at this time of year. The Scandinavian style of winter decoration with pared-back colours and a rustic, natural feel is where I take much of my inspiration. In the early part of winter I love the starkness of the winter landscape; by mid-winter I will be desperate for some colour and spring bulbs; but for now I like to use pretty twigs and pine cones to reflect the restricted colour palette of the countryside. And, if you look hard enough, there are berries, rose hips and winter flowers to add splashes of colour. This approach to Christmas decor is easy to achieve, more sustainable for the environment and hugely satisfying to create. And, at this expensive time of year, it is possible to make thrifty gifts too.

Seasonal
wreath

What you will need

- Hazel branches about 1m/39in long
- Stub or reel wire
- Wire cutters or secateurs
- Natural decorations: lichen-covered stems, larch cones, rose hips, garden moss, sweet chestnuts
- Ribbon, twine, raffia
- Scissors

TOP TIP

When forming your wreath, bear in mind that any material you add will make the ultimate size of your wreath larger than the actual base, so do not get too carried away with the size of the wreath base.

A welcoming wreath on your door has become just as much a part of decorating a home for Christmas as a tree. Take your pick from all manner of styles, from the traditional evergreen to the quirky, covered in Brussels sprouts. Many shop-bought versions feel mass-produced with their gaudy, plastic ribbons and uninspiring conifer fronds, so for something unique assemble your own. Unless you use florists' foam, wreaths made from fresh material will not last very long without water, so create these wreaths close to when you want them to look their best. Hanging them in cooler rooms or outdoors will help to extend their life. Dried-material wreaths will last indefinitely, so you can do these much earlier, before the hectic festive season starts. They will need some protection from the elements, so hang them on a sheltered door or indoors.

Making a seasonal wreath

- Loop one piece of hazel into a circle of the required diameter and secure with wire.
- Take another stem of hazel and weave around the circle.
- Repeat with several more stems starting at different points around the circle, to create a balanced shape.
- Continue weaving in stems until you have formed the desired wreath base.
- Gather together a couple of lichen-covered stems and a stem or two of larch cones, for a twiggy posy. Secure with wire. Lay on your wreath base to gauge the fit and trim to size.
- Make up enough of these posies to cover your wreath.
- Wire into place on your hazel wreath base, using subsequent posies to cover the wired base of the previous posy.
- Wire or poke into place further decorations of your choice. I worked in rose hips and pieces of vibrant green moss from my garden path.
- Finish by cutting and attaching some ribbon, twine or raffia to the wreath.

Alternative natural wreath bases

- Hazel (*Corylus*) makes a good rigid base, which is invaluable for large wreaths and if you have a lot of weighty material. It is easy enough to come across hazel in the hedgerows, but if you cannot find any try a local coppicer, who should have stems for sale. There are alternatives though.

- Willow (*Salix*) stems, for example, could be used as a substitute for hazel. Bunches of willow stems can be bought online, and there is a wide variety of coloured stems to choose from, thereby adding another dimension to your wreath design.

- A straw base like the one used for the Dried summer wreath (see page 70) and the Everlasting-flower wreath (see page 116) would work just as well for winter wreaths. You could even recycle the base from those projects.

- Silver birch (*Betula pendula*) is simple to work with, as it is very pliable and incredibly easy to bend into shapes. It also forms much looser wreaths, with little branches poking out in all directions for a very natural effect. Take a long branch, create a circle the size of your desired wreath base and then weave the rest of the stem around this circle. Take more stems and do the same. Do not be too precise about tucking in stray side branches as these add to the charm. The base of a birch wreath looks pretty enough to be very simply decorated with just a few stems of berries and holly (*Ilex*) or honesty (*Lunaria*) seed pods.

- The long stems of Virginia creeper (*Parthenocissus*) can be used in the same way as the silver birch. Cut long stems and strip any remaining leaves, create a circle and weave in the stems to build up the base.

TOP TIP

Evergreens make for a classic winter wreath, but do not feel constrained by this. Experiment with what you have stored from autumn and what inspires you in your winter garden and the countryside. Try old man's beard (*Clematis vitalba*), glycerined beech stems with their nuts still intact (see page 128), acorns, gloriously vibrant Chinese lanterns and nuts.

Look out for sweet chestnuts, which with their rich mahogany sheen look beautiful on wreaths. The base of the chestnut is soft enough to have a piece of stub wire pushed into it and it can then be conveniently wired into the wreath.

Decking
the table

Food is central to the festive celebrations and it is a treat at this time of year to be able to make a real feature of the dining table for meals with family and friends. Your table decorations do not need to be elaborate nor complicated; in fact sometimes modest ideas are the most striking. For the simplest of table decorations fill small jars, glasses or pretty ice-cream dishes with crab apples (*Malus*), cones and nuts. These are cute and do not take up a lot of space on a crowded Christmas table.

Scour your garden and the hedgerows for pretty foliage and berries. A mild winter can also mean that you may have a couple of brave, little flowers in bloom, such as primroses (*Primula vulgaris*) and hydrangeas, and do not forget winter-flowering plants such as winter honeysuckle (*Lonicera*). Pick the day before the relevant event and arrange, remembering not to create arrangements that are too tall, as these will make it difficult for guests to see each other and chat across the table. Then store somewhere cool until needed.

Table decorations can also include simple garlands of dried or fresh material and pretty napkin rings (see page 142). Forced bulbs (see page 162) look enchanting as winter decorations, but avoid strongly scented flowers for the dining table, where they can overpower the aroma of food. Also, be careful that non-edibles are not confused with food for eating, particularly if children and pets are around.

What you will need

- Foraged material: chestnuts, crab apples, cones, rose hips, old man's beard, hawthorn berries, birch, Virginia creeper, honesty seed pods
- Pretty containers: jelly moulds, jam jars, glasses, bowls, ice-cream dishes
- Flax cord, ribbon, hessian, raffia or twine for decoration
- Evergreens: rosemary, thyme, bay, viburnum, pine, silver-leaved dusty miller (*Jacobaea maritima*)
- Thin-gauge florists' wire
- Stub wire (optional)

Creating an honesty garland

Remove individual honesty seed pods with a little bit of stalk attached. Discard the outer casings. Cut a length of cord or ribbon to drape across your table. I used flax cord here for its natural feel. Starting in the centre, attach a silvery honesty seed pod to the cord with a knot; work outwards from the centre, securing further seed pods in place.

Posy napkin rings
and napkin adornments

A quick and easy way to dress a table for a special meal is by adding simple decorations to napkins. Choosing evergreen herbs with their delicious fragrance is a nice touch. Alternatively use sprigs of pine for that quintessential smell of Christmas. Work in seed heads or grasses that you collected in autumn or fresh pickings from your garden and the hedgerows.

What you will need

- Hessian ribbon
- Needle and thread
- Scissors
- Napkins
- Dried herbs, flowers and seed heads
- Thin-gauge florists' wire
- Twine, cord, ribbon or raffia
- Weeping birch stems, Virginia creeper
- Brown stub wire (optional)
- Rosemary, pine, bay, rose hips, berries

Making the stemmed napkin ring

- Make a circle using bendy birch stems or Virginia creeper. Check to see that your rolled napkin will fit through it.
- Continue wrapping the stem around the circle a few times to create your napkin holder. The circle should hold itself in place, but, if not, secure with brown stub wire.
- Decorate the front with whatever takes your fancy. I pushed a sprig of rose hips into the birch.

Making the posy-adorned ribbon napkin ring

- Take a length of hessian ribbon and stitch the ends together to create a tube into which to place the napkin.
- Make a simple posy from a few stems of herbs and secure it with thin-gauge florists' wire. Dried flowers and seed heads would work too.
- Cover the wire by wrapping with twine, cord, ribbon or raffia. You can then place your posy on top of the napkin or tie it in place.

Making the napkin adornments

- Take a sprig of rosemary or pine and bring the ends together to form a small circle.
- Secure in place with thin cord or twine, tying it in a bow.
- Place on top of your napkin.

Honesty

WHY? Although honesty (*Lunaria annua*) flowers come in shades of pink and in pure white and are pretty in spring arrangements with tulips and scented narcissi, it is for the parchment-like seed pods, with their satiny sheen, that I really grow honesty. These are perfect for Christmas crafting. Green oval pods will start to form in early summer, and as the seeds ripen the pods turn a dull brown. Hidden between these bland and boring outer casings is a moon-like disc of silvery beauty. When placed near fairy lights they will glisten.

HOW? Being a very simple plant to grow, the only thing to remember is that honesty is biennial, so it should be sown from late spring to midsummer in order to flower and produce its seed heads the following year. Sow honesty in seed trays, prick out and pot on, and then plant out into the final planting place in early autumn. A sunny or partly shady spot will be fine. You will know the pods are ready for picking when they feel dry and start to peel at the edges. Cut the stems right down at the base so you have large bunches. Then gently remove the outer seed casings yourself (it is oddly therapeutic!) and scatter the seeds in your garden. It will be too late for these to flower next year, but they will the following year. Alternatively you can leave the seed heads on the plant in the garden, and the outer seed casings will, with time, naturally fall away, thereby exposing the seeds and the inner membranes, but you risk the membranes being damaged by wind and rain and you want them to be as pristine as possible for your decorations. Once you have honesty in your garden, it is likely to self-sow.

Rosemary

WHY? Not only is rosemary (*Rosmarinus*) a must-have for cooking but it is also fantastic for adding scented foliage to arrangements. You can cut it at any time of the year, but I think it comes into its own in winter. Use it in fresh arrangements mixed with hedgerow berries and any brave, little flowers which may be lingering in the garden, or pair rosemary with cones and dried material for present decorations, wreaths and garlands.

Think ahead to maximize your choice of natural winter decorations. Grow plants such as honesty and *Scabiosa stellata* and collect interesting grasses and seed heads from late summer onwards.

HOW? Rosemary is an undemanding plant if you give it good drainage when you first plant it. It is a Mediterranean herb so needs a hot, sunny spot and hates sitting in wet soil. Add lots of crocks and stones to the bottom of a pot or planting hole and then work plenty of grit into the soil or potting compost. In areas where winters are very wet, lift herbs such as rosemary, pot them up and place them in a greenhouse or cold frame to keep them on the dry side over winter. Rosemary is also very easy to propagate. In mid- or late summer pull off some side shoots 8–10cm/3¼–4in long. Strip each shoot of its bottom few leaves, insert the prepared cuttings in a pot of multipurpose potting compost mixed with grit, and cover with a plastic bag to retain moisture. In 3–4 weeks roots should start to appear at the bottom of the pot. You can then plant each rosemary plantlet in an individual pot.

Bay

WHY? Evergreens have played a part in winter celebrations in the northern hemisphere for thousands of years. They are steeped in superstition and folklore – our ancestors were fascinated about these plants' ability to stay green throughout winter, and as a result they have become intrinsically linked with Christmas decoration. Bay (*Laurus nobilis*) is a classic evergreen that imparts a lovely aroma when used in decorations and can also be enjoyed fresh or dried in cooking.

HOW? Bay can reach 7.5m/25ft if grown in the ground, yet it will thrive in a large pot. In both situations it is easy to keep smaller by pruning it. Having originated from the Mediterranean, it thrives in a warm, sheltered spot. It can suffer in very cold winters so the advantage of growing bay in a pot is that you can move it into a porch or greenhouse for the winter months or cover it more easily with horticultural fleece. Bay needs well-drained soil, so plant it in John Innes soil-based compost with added grit if growing it in a container. Repot every two years and feed every few weeks during the growing season with liquid seaweed fertilizer.

Deciduous
branch tree

Early winter storms can often bring down branches, cones and lichen, which are perfect for creating your own take on a Christmas tree. A tree branch of contorted hazel (*Corylus avellana* 'Contorta'), birch (*Betula*), alder (*Alnus*) or a tree with a similarly good structure and shape on which to hang decorations is a great alternative to a typical festive evergreen tree of Norway spruce (*Picea abies*) or noble fir (*Abies procera*). Birch makes a good natural tree, and alder already comes with tiny cones attached. I love to have a few stems of contorted hazel with its twisted stems gathered together. Just a branch of such a tree is ideal if your living space is small and is a thrifty option. It is also an excellent choice if you would like an extra festive tree – perhaps in a dining room or child's bedroom. A wide-bottomed container is good as it will be very stable. A tall, galvanized florists' bucket also works well, giving the stems plenty of support. Alternatively a tall, plastic clematis or rose pot would do.

I love the twisted, curly stems of contorted hazel when decorated with natural baubles of Billy buttons, crab apples, Chinese lanterns and *Scabiosa stellata*.

✂ What you will need

- Branches of birch, alder or contorted hazel
- Secateurs
- Pretty, tall container or one with a wide, flat bottom
- Pine cones and (optional) hessian and twine for decoration
- Pebbles
- Newspaper

Preparing a deciduous branch tree

- Look for a tree that has branches with lots of side shoots, on which to hang your decorations. Cut off the branch and if necessary prune it to fit your space, but be careful not to spoil the natural shape of the piece you have chosen.
- Then choose your container. I used an old sweet jar with a wide bottom and added pine cones around the stems to add an extra seasonal touch; they also helped to wedge the stems into place in an attractive way. Alternatively try a tall, galvanized florists' bucket or a plastic pot disguised with a wrapping of hessian tied in place with twine.
- Tall containers with a narrow base can be prone to toppling over, so fill around the base of the stem with pebbles to weigh it down. Then stuff some newspaper in around the branch-tree stem to hold it in place. Hide the top of the newspaper with a layer of pine cones.

Natural
baubles

What you will need

- Crochet hook (optional)
- Raffia, twine or natural cord such as hemp
- Natural decorations: Billy buttons, *Scabiosa stellata*, Chinese lanterns, acorns, beech nuts, larch cones, honesty, crab apples, hops

These are the perfect complement to your deciduous branch tree (see page 146) and continue the rustic, woodland feel. The combination of the branch tree and decorations is ideal if, like me, you are wanting to decorate the house by the start of December but know a live evergreen tree will not last until Christmas Day if you put it up so early.

Making natural baubles

If you can crochet, create a short chain using hemp cord and attach it to each decoration. Secure each ornament to the tree by the top loop of the chain. If you do not want to crochet, attach each using a bow of raffia, twine or hemp.

Skeletonizing foliage

A skeleton leaf is simply the framework of the leaf – the veins and ribs – that has been left behind once the fleshy skin of the leaf has been eroded. You might be lucky enough to come across leaves where this process has occurred naturally, as a result of appropriate weather conditions, bacteria and organisms breaking down the skin. It is possible though to replicate this process yourself by filling a small bucket with rainwater and placing the leaves into it and soaking them for a period of time. Thinner material will take a few weeks; thicker leaves such as magnolia may need a few months. Some foliage is more successful than others – magnolia and holly (*Ilex*) being particularly good. This same technique can be used on Chinese lanterns and poppy seed heads.

Foraged
fairy

A collection of finds from the garden and from woodland walks were combined to produce this sweet, little fairy. The body is a pine cone. To create a spot for the head to rest on, snip out the top point of the cone. For the head, secure an acorn in place using a glue gun. Top off the head with a beech nut seed pod. For the fairy's wings, glue on sycamore seed pods. Cut down thin branches to make arms. Finally give the fairy a skirt by gluing a Chinese lantern to the base of the pine cone. Carefully snip along the sides of the lantern from the base to about one-third of the way up, to open the lantern so it looks more skirt-like. Attach a length of cord to the back of the pine cone, then hang the fairy from your tree. If you do not have Chinese lanterns, try colourful autumn leaves to form the skirt.

✂ What you will need

- Pine cone, acorn, beech nut seed pod, sycamore seed pods, thin deciduous branches, Chinese lantern or colourful autumn leaves
- Scissors
- Hot-glue gun
- Secateurs
- Cord

Pine cones are essential for winter crafting. Wire them into wreaths, hang from your tree, use to decorate presents or display them on their own.

Billy buttons

WHY? This native of Australia and New Zealand is a new-found favourite of mine. The tiny flowers of Billy buttons (*Craspedia*) form a tightly packed, golden globe with no typical petals to be seen. They are such striking flowers that I like to display them on their own through the summer and autumn, although the main reason for Billy buttons becoming such a favourite is that they can be dried and they retain their colouring.

HOW? Sow from early to mid-spring and plant out once it is warm enough in late spring. Billy buttons can be slow growers so sowing early and nurturing indoors will provide you with flowers by midsummer. Glaucous green clumps of leaves will form and long, straight stems 20–30cm/8–12in tall will appear with a single flower on top. If you cut the stems close to the base, new flowering stems will subsequently emerge. Dry the flowers by hanging upside down in a warm, dark and dry place. They will take about ten days to dry fully. Although a perennial in its native lands, Billy buttons would normally be treated as an annual in cool-temperate areas in the northern hemisphere, but it is worth trying to get it through a winter, either by mulching if you live in a frost-free spot or by digging up the plant, putting it in a pot and keeping it somewhere sheltered such as a greenhouse or cold frame before planting out again in spring.

Chinese lanterns

WHY? The hardy perennial Chinese lantern (*Physalis alkekengi*), with its papery, orange lanterns which protect the seed inside, is the plant to grow if you are interested in natural decoration. It produces nondescript, small, white flowers, with the orange seed pods appearing from early autumn. The pods retain their striking, orange colouring when preserved by cutting stems from the main plant and standing them in a container – you do not need to fill it with water – somewhere warm and dry and out of direct sunlight. Seed pods can also be left on the plant, where they will fade to leave delightful golden skeletons encasing the orange fruits.

HOW? It is possible to grow Chinese lanterns from seed but they can be sourced as mature plants at most garden centres or nurseries. Plants establish readily, perhaps a little too readily, so it is best to confine their roots to a large pot or raised bed. They are unfussy perennials, thriving in most conditions other than shade. The variety you are most likely to come across is *P.a.* var. *franchetii*, which grows to about 75cm/30in in height.

Crab apples

WHY? Even the smallest of gardens should have a tree, but choosing a plant that will be a long-term feature requires some thought, particularly if space is tight and you want something that will look good throughout the year. Crab apples (*Malus*) are one of the best trees as they produce stunning spring blossom, a lovely green backdrop during summer and autumn leaf colour as well as miniature apples. If you select the right variety, these fruits can remain on the tree well into winter. My own crab apple is M. 'Evereste', which has delightful blossom – tight, pink buds open into white flowers with the most lovely scent, like freshly washed linen. In autumn the leaves turn a golden colour and the green fruits start to ripen, with hints of red forming. As the leaves drop, the red fruits 'drip' from the tree, brightening up a corner in my garden. The fruit on M. 'Evereste' will remain on the tree into mid-winter. This cultivar will reach about 6m/20ft when mature, with a similar spread, and it will take 10–15 years to do this, making it a good choice for many gardens. Crab apples are not edible straight from the tree – they are much too sour – but they can be made into beautifully coloured apple jelly. Crab apple trees are also fabulous for wildlife. In spring, they will be a humming mass of bees, which will dine on the blossom. Birds will love to rest on them and will be grateful for the fruits as a source of food in winter. An established crab apple will also be host to all manner of insects and so is perfect for increasing the biodiversity in your garden.

HOW? Late autumn to mid-spring are the best times to plant a tree, as long as the ground is not frosted or waterlogged. Dig a planting hole that is about three times the diameter of the root ball and the same depth as the roots. Loosen the soil at the base to break up any compaction. Sprinkle mycorrhizal fungi on to the roots of the tree and into the planting hole as per the instructions on the packet. The fungi will help your tree to become established. Place the tree in the hole and backfill carefully. Gently firm the soil around the tree. In windy or exposed sites and for large specimens, insert a stake to provide stability for the tree in its first years, and tie the tree to it. Water generously, and make sure that the tree does not suffer from stress caused by a lack of water during the first few years after planting.

The miniature fruits of a crab apple tree look beautiful when wired into wreaths, dangling from your branch tree. Or you could fill pretty glasses and bowls with them to decorate your dining table.

Larch-cone
mini wreath

✂ What you will need

- Compass and pencil
- Cardboard – a cereal box is perfect
- Scissors
- Twine or ribbon to hang the wreath
- PVA glue and a spatula or old butter knife
- Newspaper
- Hot-glue gun
- Foraged goodies such as larch cones, acorns and bits from your autumn store of poppy seed heads, love-in-a-mist and *Scabiosa stellata*

If you remember making papier mâché as a child you will enjoy creating these simple decorations. Take inspiration from the seed heads you have stored from the summer and autumn and collect pine cones, acorns and beech nuts from your local wood or park. Hang these from your Christmas tree or combine a few to decorate a door or wall. You can scale up your design to make larger decorations, but you may need a base of stronger cardboard than the cereal packet used here. The newspaper balls will give your cardboard rings a curved profile so that your finished decoration will have a fuller appearance and there will be no gaps between the cones.

I used larch cones for this project, but you could try acorns or sweet chestnuts. The seed heads of poppies, love-in-a-mist and *Scabiosa stellata* would work too and make unique decorations.

Forming the ring shape

Using a compass and pencil, draw a circle 5.5cm/2¼in in diameter on the cardboard. Then pencil another, smaller concentric circle, inside the first and about 2.5cm/1in in diameter. Cut out this central circle to leave a ring of cardboard. Make two of these rings.

Take a piece of ribbon or twine for hanging your decoration and double it over. Glue the two ends together on to the back ring – if you are using cardboard with text on it place these sides on what will be the inside of your decoration. Then take the second ring and glue in place, making a cardboard 'sandwich'.

Padding the base

Tear off pieces of newspaper and roll up into small balls. Use a dab of the PVA glue to stop the balls unravelling and then glue them to the cardboard ring.

Finishing the base

Continue making and glueing balls until you have covered the ring. Coat all the balls with a layer of PVA glue. This will harden to form a base on to which you will secure your foraged finds.

Attaching the cones

Leave the ring to dry for a day or so. Then, using a hot-glue gun, attach larch cones, acorns or poppy seed heads to the newspaper balls.

Natural
present decoration

If you despair at the pile of discarded wrappings on Christmas Day that cannot be recycled or you do not like plastic, shiny bows and ribbon, then turn to something more natural. Use plain white and brown parcel paper to wrap presents and adorn them with natural ornaments. This honesty and poppy seed-head flower is quite delicate so is best for gifts that you will deliver in person. There are plenty of alternative decorative materials such as small leaves, which can be attached around the base of a larch cone.

What you will need

- Scissors or secateurs
- Dried seed heads of poppy and honesty
- Hot-glue gun
- Twine or pretty ribbon
- Small, autumn-coloured leaves, such as those of blueberries
- Larch cones

Making a natural present decoration

- Snip off the stem of a dried poppy, leaving 1cm/½in of stem with the seed head attached.
- Remove honesty membranes from their seed-pod casings and, with a dab of glue at the base of each, attach around the poppy seed head to form a flower. You can do just one row or add more for a fuller effect.
- Attach the decoration to your present with the twine or ribbon you have used in the wrapping. You can add a dab of glue if you want to make sure that the decoration stays in place. The honesty membranes are very delicate, so bare this in mind when attaching to your present.

TOP TIPS

If you do not have any honesty or you find it too delicate, decorate your gifts with other seed pods (such as love-in-a-mist) and grasses (such as hare's tail). Try cones or sprigs of berries. Bay leaves and rosemary look pretty too.

Lichen
star

These lichen stars would look lovely hanging on a wall or from a door. Small ones could be suspended from a tree. They are incredibly thrifty and easy decorations to assemble. Their creation provides the perfect excuse to get out for a winter's walk and gather some inspiring objects from your local wood. Collect a selection of pretty windfall branches covered in lichen or moss. Try to find ones that are relatively straight, as this will give more definition to the final shape. If you store your lichen star in an old shoebox it will last for years, or you could just leave it in place in your house. Mine has been hanging from a door in my kitchen for several years. And when it is looking a little shabby I will remove the wire and pop the lichen star on to the compost heap.

Making a lichen star

Cut the branches into six equal lengths. The twigs for this star measured 23cm/9in, but you can make them larger or smaller. Arrange the branches into two equilateral triangles and secure each corner with brown stub wire. You can then bind each side with hemp cord, for a neater finish. Place one triangle on top of the other and use hemp cord to secure the triangles together at the points where they cross. Hang with natural twine or hemp cord.

HOW TO:
Force bulbs

By forcing bulbs you bring them into flower earlier than they would normally. There are plenty of bulbs that can be treated in this way, and they offer a great alternative to the ubiquitous poinsettias, which fill our garden centres and supermarkets every winter.

The easiest and classiest of bulbs to force for winter decoration has to be paper-white narcissus (*Narcissus papyraceous*). The most commonly sold variety is *N.p.* 'Ziva', although there are others such as *N.p.* 'Inbal'. Paper-whites have multi-headed stems with delicate, pure white flowers with the most incredible fragrance. Unlike the narcissi grown in gardens, paper-whites are tender varieties originating from the eastern Mediterranean so they are not suitable for growing outdoors in cool-temperate areas. Fortunately they are easy to bring into flower for an indoor display. Bulbs of paper-white narcissi tend to become available from late summer, and you can plant at regular intervals from then right up until mid-winter. They generally take 6–8 weeks between planting and flowering, but if you plant in late summer you can have flowers after only four weeks. Once you have bought your bulbs they will be desperate to grow, so if you do not want to use them immediately store the bulbs somewhere cool and dark but frost-free. You can put them in the bottom of

> Plan ahead for winter flowers by planting bulbs for forcing in late summer and early autumn. Try amaryllis (*Hippeastrum*), paper-white narcissi and specially treated hyacinths.

your refrigerator to retard growth. When you bring them out, condensation will form on the bulbs because of the change in temperature, so allow them to dry out a little before you plant, to prevent them from becoming mouldy.

There are also all sorts of other bulbs that can be grown to provide winter cheer. Amaryllis (*Hippeastrum*) comes in a great range of colours and looks incredibly exotic. For scent, buy specially treated hyacinth bulbs for forcing, which will come into bloom early. Plant up crocuses and early-flowering dwarf and Cyclamineus narcissi, keeping them in a greenhouse or cold frame and then bringing them indoors to bloom in late winter. With a selection of bulbs planted at regular intervals it is possible to have a succession of flowers from autumn right through to spring.

If your chosen pot does not have any drainage holes, add a layer of grit about 2.5cm/1in deep to the bottom of the pot so that plant roots will not sit in waterlogged compost.

PLANTING FORCED BULBS

You can grow your forced bulbs in bulb fibre or potting compost mixed with some biochar (see page 29) to keep the potting medium smelling fresh. They can be planted in all manner of pretty containers. Once planted, store somewhere cool and dark for a week or so to allow the roots to develop. Bring out and place somewhere sunny to maximize the amount of light they receive. Water only when the compost feels dry and try not to overwater.

Add grit to the bottom of any pot without drainage holes.

Fill the container with multipurpose compost mixed with a little biochar, or use bulb fibre.

Pack the bulbs into the pot, pushing them down so the bases are in contact with the compost.

BULBS IN WATER

Both paper-white narcissi and hyacinths can also be grown in just water, with the bulb resting on a bed of pebbles or shells placed in the bottom of a container. Pour in enough water so that it settles just below the base of the bulb; the roots will sense the water and reach down into it. If the bulb is in contact with the water it can rot. Top up the water as necessary. Start off the bulbs somewhere cool and dark for a week or so, to allow the roots to develop, then bring out into as a sunny a position as possible. Low light levels can make the bulbs grow leggy and floppy. A pretty nest of woven birch twigs can provide some support.

PAPER-WHITE NARCISSI IN WATER AND ALCOHOL

Another forcing technique is to grow paper-white narcissi in a mixture of water and alcohol. The flowers and foliage have a tendency to strain for the light and become leggy, but studies in the USA have shown that growing the bulbs in an alcohol solution stunts the growth of the plant with no impact on the quality of the flowers, and my own experience backs this up. To use the alcohol method, grow your bulbs initially in water as mentioned (left), over a base of pebbles. Once the roots have established and the shoot has turned green and is about 2.5cm/1in tall, gently tip out the water and replace it with an alcohol–water mix, keeping it away from the base of the bulb. I make up a bottle of the mix comprising one part gin or vodka to seven parts water and use this to top up the liquid level as needed. Do not introduce a stronger solution or other types of alcoholic drink such as wine, because both will damage the plants.

Frosting

- -

Much as I love natural Christmas decorations, I do crave a bit of sparkle now and again. If you prefer not to resort to cans of spray paint, which mean you cannot compost your winter decorations once you have finished with them, then try the technique of frosting to add a touch of natural glitter to your decorations. Having been long included in baking for pretty cake decorations, the idea is perfect too for use at Christmas. Make sure guests, especially children, understand that these frosted items are for decoration and that they are not to be eaten. Fruits such as pears and pomegranates are the classic frosted table decoration, but you could look for something in your garden, the hedgerows or from the bits and pieces you have gathered over the previous months. Use the frosted items to create a table centrepiece or place settings. Make pieces to decorate presents or cover your natural baubles for your deciduous branch tree (see page 146). If you are wanting to frost fruits or berries, do this as close to when you need them as possible and store them somewhere cool.

What you will need
- Egg
- Bowl
- Fork
- 50–60g/1½–2oz white caster sugar
- Tray or plate
- Small paintbrush
- Leaves and berries for decorating: bay, rosemary, pine, rose hips, hawthorn berries, crab apples
- Nonstick baking paper

APPLYING THE FROSTING
- Separate the egg yolk from the egg white. Then, using a fork, lightly beat the egg white in a bowl.
- Spread out the caster sugar on the tray or plate. You can use granulated sugar, but the larger grains will give a less refined finish.
- With the paintbrush, cover your leaves and berries in a thin layer of egg white.
- Then press them in the caster sugar, until they are evenly coated. You are aiming to capture the look of a light dusting of frost – not something covered in snow!
- Shake off any excess and place on a sheet of baking paper. Do not use kitchen paper because you will end up with bits of paper stuck to your leaves and berries when you peel them off.
- Place in the refrigerator until you want to use the frosted items.

If you feel the sugar coating is too thick, wash it off and dry your leaf or berry thoroughly before starting again.

Favoured resources

FLORISTRY SUPPLIES

Most online floristry suppliers sell only wholesale or in very large quantities, but you can purchase wire and floral tape from florists and garden centres and from Fred Aldous (see above).

The Baggery Group sells all manner of floristry sundries and provides excellent service: www.thebaggery.co.uk

If you want to supplement your home-grown plant material with extra flowers, **British Flower Collective** and **Flowers from the Farm** both have online directories where you can search for British flower growers near you: www.thebritishflowercollective.com www.flowersfromthefarm.co.uk

For hot-glue guns I use a **Puregadgets** 20W electric glue gun (available online).

GENERAL CRAFTING

Fred Aldous is crafting heaven. There is an excellent website supported by great service, and if you happen to be in Manchester there is a shop (37 Lever Street, Manchester M1 1LW) which is a treasure trove. You name it, it is sold by Fred Aldous, from ready-made flower presses to the cardboard and blotting paper you need to make your own press; from hemp cord and florists' wire to everything you might require for your crafting toolbox: www.fredaldous.co.uk

Isca Woodcrafts is a brilliant place for wood-related projects with a wide range of native and non-native woods available. The workshop is at The Crafts Units, Tredegar House, Newport NP10 8TW: www.iscawoodcrafts.co.uk

HABERDASHERY

Lancaster & Cornish sell gorgeous haberdashery and fabrics. I particularly love the range of hand-dyed, organic-silk ribbons, which use dyes created from plants and flowers, some of which are grown by Cornish flower farmers and florists Becca and Maz: www.lancasterandcornish.com www.thegardengateflowercompany.co.uk

The Makery is a delightful shop (Beau Nash House, 19 Union Passage, Bath BA1 1RD), in which you will find a plethora of ribbons, buttons and cool fabrics. The company does mail order too: http://themakery.co.uk

Mill Pond Flower Farm also sell a range of hand-dyed silk ribbons using natural dyes from the Scottish countryside: http://www.millpondflowerfarm.co.uk

Nutscene has a great choice of jute twines in a rainbow of colours. Their twines are not just useful in the garden because I also choose them all the time when crafting. I even crochet with twine. Nutscene also sells hessian ribbon: http://nutscene.com

RE sells an eclectic mix of beautiful homewares. I particularly love the grey flax cord. There are two shops (Bishops Yard, Main Street, Corbridge NE45 5LA; and in the BALTIC Centre for Contemporary Art, Gateshead NE8 3BA) as well as a website: www.re-foundobjects.com

Hessian is a woven fabric made from jute. It is fabulous for crafting and is easy to find. Try a local fabric shop, the haberdashery section of John Lewis (www.johnlewis.com) or online.

PAPER

Khadi has great environmental and social credentials. The website sells hemp string and a fantastic selection of acid-free papers made from waste cotton, jute, banana leaves and sugar cane fibre:
http://khadi.com

PaperWorks stocks a fabulous selection of papers from around the world. It has a shop (63 High Street, Totnes, Devon TQ9 5PB) as well as a good website:
www.paperworks.uk.com

PLANTS

Alpines
Most garden centres will have a good selection of alpines from early to mid-spring, but to find a greater range of plants try a specialist alpine nursery such as:
Ice Alpines www.icealpines.co.uk
Gordon's Nursery www.gordonsnursery.co.uk

Bulbs
Buying bulbs from a specialist supplier means you have a much greater choice, as well as bulbs that have been stored correctly:
Peter Nyssen www.peternyssen.com
Avon Bulbs www.avonbulbs.co.uk
R.A. Scamp www.qualitydaffodils.com

Chrysanthemums
Specialist growers such as the following have a wide selection of varieties:
Woolmans www.woolmans.com
Chrysanthemums Direct
www.chrysanthemumsdirect.co.uk

Dahlias
For good-sized tubers at great prices try the following. They all stock the 'Karma' varieties, which are perfect for cut flowers:
Peter Nyssen www.peternyssen.com
National Dahlia Collection
www.national-dahlia-collection.co.uk
Rose Cottage Plants
www.rosecottageplants.co.uk

Dried flowers
If you want to buy extra dried flowers, there are some fantastic companies online that sell British-grown dried flowers. Try:
Winter Flora www.winterflora.com
Broome Beck Flower Farm
www.thedriedflowerfarm.co.uk

Herbs
For a comprehensive selection of herbs, try a specialist nursery such as the following, which both stock English mace (*Achillea ageratum*):
Hooksgreen Herbs www.hooksgreenherbs.com
Cooks Lane Herbs http://cookslaneherbs.co.uk

Hops
For dried hops, hop plants and a selection of dried flowers, try:
Essentially Hops www.essentiallyhops.co.uk

Scented plants
Whether for keeping alive old varieties or for breeding fantastic new ones, try these for a good selection of scented pinks:
Whetman Pinks www.whetmanpinks.com
Lavender Blue www.lavenderandpinks.co.uk
Allwoods www.allwoods.net

Succulents
Most good garden centres will have a small range of succulents, but for more unusual varieties try online specialists:
Surreal Succulents www.surrealsucculents.co.uk
Fernwood Nursery www.fernwood-nursery.co.uk

Terrarium plants
For a selection of hostas, ferns and mosses which will thrive in the high humidity and low light levels of a terrarium try the following:
Bowdens Hostas www.bowdenhostas.com
Mickfield Hostas www.mickfieldhostas.co.uk
Kelways www.kelways.co.uk

Wild flowers and native plants
I much prefer the idea of picking wild flowers from my own garden rather than being tempted to cut them in the wild (which is illegal for some plants). There are some great nurseries out there specializing in native, wild

plants where you can be sure they have been propagated responsibly. Try:

PlantWild http://plantwild.co.uk
Wild Thyme Plants www.wildthymeplants.co.uk

POTTING SUPPLIES

Biochar

For biochar from sustainably managed woodlands, try:
www.dorsetcharcoal.co.uk
www.carbongold.com

Potting composts

Vital Earth offers an excellent range of potting composts, including peat-free, soil-based John Innes ones, which are ideal for plants that will be in containers for longer than a few months. For a list of stockists, look on its website:
http://thegreenergardener.com

SEEDS

Chiltern Seeds offers an extensive collection of cut-flower and grass seeds:
www.chilternseeds.co.uk

Higgledy Garden offers a great range of cut-flower seeds with a personal level of service you will not find elsewhere. Handwritten letters with your seed delivery no less:
http://higgledygarden.com

The Organic Gardening Catalogue sells pretty much everything you might need for the garden, with an emphasis on gardening sustainably and providing a good choice of vegetable and flower seeds. It is also where you will find wheatgrass seeds for the Spring in a teacup project (see page 46):
www.organiccatalogue.com

Seek out specialist plant nurseries and seed suppliers for greater choice and expert knowledge.

Otter Farm has a fantastic selection of attractive edibles. Try the scented-leaved pelargonium collection and the microgreens:
www.otterfarm.co.uk

Sarah Raven For cut-flower seeds, plug plants, vegetables and bulbs – you will be seduced by the vibrant selection in Sarah Raven's catalogues and online:
www.sarahraven.com

Suttons Seeds has a comprehensive collection of seeds, both floral and edible:
www.suttons.co.uk

VINTAGE FINDS

A perfect pot or unusual container can make all the difference when displaying your plants or cutting material. You do not need to spend a lot of money or resort to modern, mass-manufactured products, though. Flea markets and charity shops are the ideal places to come across a piece of pretty china or metal tray, or you could try the growing number of online companies that will do the legwork for you.

The Balcony Gardener stocks a good selection of containers, both new and old, including old medicine bottles and large glass containers, which are ideal for creating a terrarium:
www.thebalconygardener.com

Petersham Nurseries is a treasure trove of gardenalia and homewares, as well as a source of plants. I could spend hours mooching around this place. Try their online store or visit the nursery (Church Lane, off Petersham Road, Richmond, Surrey TW10 7AB):
http://petershamnurseries.com

The following all specialize in vintage home and gardenware:
The Foodie Bugle Shop
www.thefoodiebugleshop.com
Loop the Loop www.looptheloop.co.uk
Mabel & Rose www.mabelandrose.com

Index

Acknowledgments

A huge 'thank you' to the team at Frances Lincoln, in particular to Helen, Becky and Joanna for your creativity and patience.

Jason, thank you once again for taking such stunning photographs. As always it has been a pleasure to work with you.

Many thanks to Loop the Loop, Kelways, Mickfield Hostas, Bowdens Hostas, Suttons Seeds, CB Imports, The Balcony Gardener, RE, The Makery and Fred Aldous for your generosity.

To Doug Williams, Bob at Isca Woodcrafts and Richard Hayward for your help and advice.

To Bob and Karen Millar for your help and Rhiannon for your nimble stitching.

To Karen Lynes at Peter Nyssen for such generosity with your time and knowledge.

To my friends in the world of blogging, Twitter and Instagram, thank you for the welcome distraction.

To my fabulous friend Sara and her lovely mum Ann, thank you for your support and kindness, and thank you to Tony for feeding us while we talked flowers.

To Mary for sharing your spider plants with a stranger.

To Maggie Biss and John Hagon for coming to the rescue.

To the delightful British flower growers: Justine Scouller of Farhill Flowers, Monmouthshire; Heather Brennan of Flora & Herb, Monmouthshire; and Jo and Wendy at Organic Blooms, Bristol.

To my sister-in-law Liz for making the lovely hand warmers on page 17 at such short notice.

A special thank you to Lucy. I will always be immensely grateful to you for giving me the opportunity to write for you.

To my mum and dad for encouraging my love of crafting from an early age.

And to Ian. What can I say? Thank you for your never-ending support and your determination to make everything possible – you are the best.

Photographic acknowledgments

All images in this book are by Jason Ingram except for the following, which were taken by Ian Curley:
Pages 20–21, 24–5, 26 (top left), 27 (top right), 29–30, 40, 44–5, 48, 59, 62–3, 65 (bottom right), 68–9, 74–5, 80–81, 100–101, 104–5, 108–9, 112–13, 118–19, 122–3, 144–5, 152–3.

Collect allium seed heads in summer and early autumn before they are damaged by stormy weather.